Foreword

Conflict is a part of everyday life. Unfortunately, many people lack the skills to resolve conflict fairly. Teaching children conflict resolution skills cannot only turn conflict into a positive experience for everyone involved, it can also create a caring school atmosphere, promote problem-solving skills and encourage peace.

The practical activities in *Conflict Resolution* will help children understand how to resolve conflict successfully, and allow them to practise skills and strategies to COMMUNICATE, NEGOTIATE and CONSOLIDATE conflict resolution procedures.

Titles in this series:

Conflict Resolution – Lower Primary
Conflict Resolution – Middle Primary
Conflict Resolution – Upper Primary
Conflict Resolution and Bullying – Lower Secondary

Contents

Teachers notes

Each student page is supported by a teachers page which provides the following information.

The **drama icon** indicates the inclusion of a drama activity. Drama is an excellent medium for work on conflict resolution.

Specific **objectives** explain what the students are expected to demonstrate through completing the activities.

Teacher information provides the teacher with detailed additional information to supplement the student page. Teaching points are also included where appropriate.

An **additional activity** has been included where appropriate.

Discussion points have been suggested to further develop ideas on the student page.

Curriculum Links list the curriculum objectives covered by the activity.

On some teacher pages a space has been provided for any **additional notes** the teacher may require, such as reference material or personal information on real-life incidents.

What is conflict resolution?

Conflict resolution is a process that directs responsibility for solving a conflict to the people involved. Clear steps are followed to achieve a solution that suits both parties. These are:

- defining the problem,
- brainstorming possible solutions,
- agreeing on the best solution,
- putting the best solution into action.

In schools, students faced with opposing viewpoints will often go to a teacher to sort out a conflict and decide on a solution. Instead, students should be encouraged to use conflict resolution to resolve minor conflicts such as name-calling, rumours, taking property without asking, teasing and invading personal space. The conflict resolution process teaches students that conflict need not be a negative experience, but can motivate change and provide opportunities.

This book helps students to understand conflict resolution steps, comprehend, analyse and solve conflict resolution scenarios, gain an understanding of the consequences of actions during conflict, explore conflict in history, and use role-play to problem-solve and identify feelings during conflict.

What is peer mediation?

Peer mediation is used when conflicting parties have tried to solve a conflict on their own but cannot agree on a fair solution. A neutral third student is then asked to help.

Peer mediation should only be attempted in a school where staff and students have attended a training course. As not all students have the personality to be effective mediators, students who are to be trained in the process should be chosen carefully.

Peer mediators are trained to:
- use conflict resolution steps to help two people solve a problem,
- listen to both sides of the story,
- use a consistent approach to solving problems,
- be impartial,
- attack the problem, rather than the people involved,
- encourage the conflicting parties to treat each other with respect.

This book helps students to understand and use mediation steps, how to use compromise, understand where mediation should take place and evaluate mediation situations in which they have been involved.

Peer mediation is still in its infancy in terms of widespread practice in the UK and Ireland, but is used extensively in the USA and Australia.

CONFLICT RESOLUTION

Prim-Ed Publishing
www.prim-ed.com

0582C–09/03

Conflict Resolution—Middle Primary
Prim-Ed Publishing

Published in 2003 by R.I.C. Publications
Reprinted under license in 2003 by Prim-Ed Publishing

Copyright R.I.C. Publications 2003

ISBN 1 86400 779 6
PR–0582

Additional titles available in this series:
Conflict Resolution—Lower Primary
Conflict Resolution—Upper Primary
Bullying and Conflict Resolution—Secondary
Conflict Resolution Poster Set

Prim-Ed Publishing Pty Ltd

Home Page: http://www.prim-ed.com
Email: sales@prim-ed.com

Teachers notes

What is negotiation?

Negotiation is the problem-solving process used to resolve conflict. The goal of negotiation is to create a solution the conflicting parties agree to.

Before a negotiation meeting, the people involved should think carefully about what they will say. The parties then meet in a quiet, neutral place; e.g. a 'negotiating table' in a corner of the classroom. The conflict is identified and an agreement to resolve it is made.

An important part of the negotiation process is using 'I' statements to describe wants and needs. When describing wants and needs, students should speak calmly and give reasons. When listening to someone else, they should demonstrate active listening through positive feedback and eye contact.

Effective negotiation relies on clear communication, problem-solving skills, showing respect and a focus on finding a 'win-win' solution.

Focus on the problem, not the person.

This book helps students to understand the steps that should be used during negotiation, express their needs and wants, understand what makes a good negotiator and write a negotiating play script.

What skills and attitudes should be fostered?

For conflict resolution to be effective in a class or school, certain skills and attitudes are necessary. The following skills and attitudes are a focus of the activities in this book.

• Empathy and tolerance

Conflict is often caused by a lack of understanding of others. Empathy and tolerance should therefore be encouraged in students. Activities that require students to put themselves in someone else's place and imagine how they feel can help to foster empathy. Tolerance is an on-going process that teaches children not to hate. Teachers can teach tolerance most effectively by modelling tolerant behaviour in the classroom and playground, ensuring students are exposed to multicultural literature and images, and teaching them about various faiths, ethnicities and lifestyles. Educating students to be tolerant will:

- promote the understanding and acceptance of individual differences,
- promote the idea that differences can enhance our relationships and enrich our society,
- minimise generalisations and stereotyping,
- promote the need to combat prejudice and discrimination.

Students will learn about empathy and tolerance in this book through activities that help them recognise prejudice and understand other students in their class.

A core belief creates blindspots so it's important to really hear the other person's story.

Teachers notes

• Communication skills

Speaking and listening skills are vital to prevent and resolve conflicts. Students should be encouraged to speak clearly and calmly and use eye contact, particularly when involved in negotiation. The role-play activities in this book provide students with opportunities to practise these skills. Active listening also needs to be learnt and practised because people involved in conflict often fail to interpret correctly what others are saying.

Students will explore the value of good communication in this book through activities that help them to recognise a good listener, understand passive, assertive and aggressive communication and use 'I' statements correctly.

Communication is an expression of thought. Barriers such as anger can lead to that communication not being received. It's hard to accept anything from someone when angry. It is important to cushion a person's emotions when negotiating a solution.

• Teamwork

The ability to work with others towards a common goal is a vital conflict resolution skill that can be practised in a range of curriculum areas. The following qualities are necessary for a team to function at its best:

- working towards a clear goal – the team clearly understands and works towards the goal that is to be achieved.

- good communication – the team members listen to each other with respect and willingly share their ideas without domination.

- consideration – the team members encourage and support each other's ideas, giving critical feedback.

Students will learn about teamwork in this book through activities that allow them to participate in team-building, evaluate their teamwork and discover the qualities of a good team.

• Problem-solving

Students should become familiar with problem-solving steps to solve conflict. The following steps should be taught:

- define the problem,

- brainstorm possible solutions,

- evaluate the ideas,

- decide on a solution and carry it out.

Students will explore problem-solving in this book through activities that require them to use the steps described above.

• Anger management

It is important for teachers to create an atmosphere in their classrooms that allows students to express and manage angry feelings. This can be done by ensuring that all rules are clear, fair and consistent, adopting anger management strategies for certain students, and modelling positive anger management strategies such as taking a deep breath, getting away from the situation that is causing the anger, trying to relax, or self-talk.

Students will learn about anger management in this book through activities that help them to recognise suitable and unsuitable reactions to conflict.

• Peacemaking

The goal of peacemaking is to ensure that all people are able to fully enjoy their human rights. For students to be effective peacemakers, they should have an understanding of what peace is, its importance and how they can create it. To begin with, they should understand that peace is not a passive state (a lack of war), but a process which relies on communication and action to be created and sustained. Teachers should emphasise resolving conflicts at all levels to reach a peaceful solution where everyone wins.

Students will learn about the value of peace in this book through activities that help them to reflect on what peace means and by finding peaceful solutions to situations.

Teachers notes

How can conflict resolution be implemented in a classroom or school?

Schools that have implemented conflict resolution programmes report that conflicts are being handled more quickly, physical fighting is declining and more caring behaviour is shown.

The first step in implementing conflict resolution programmes is to create a cooperative classroom and school environment where rules, rights and responsibilities are clearly stated, and where students feel able to say what they feel. The school should also hold the belief that social skills are as important as academic skills.

Teachers can also:

- teach or encourage the skills and attitudes covered in 'What skills and attitudes should be fostered?'

- inform parents of conflict resolution steps. Ask them to support the programmes by encouraging their children to use conflict resolution steps to solve problems at home,

- introduce mediation training courses for students and staff (Details of mediation courses can be found on the Internet. Try typing 'school mediation courses' into a search engine.),

- teach students how to deliver 'I' statements correctly,

- hang charts with conflict resolution steps in the classroom and around the school,

- create a 'negotiating corner' in the classroom.

Curriculum Links

Country	Year/Group	Subject	Curriculum Strand	Content Objectives
England	KS2 (Y3/4)	PSHE and Citizenship	2a	• research, discuss and debate problems and events
			2c	• realise the consequences of anti-social and aggressive behaviours, such as bullying and racism
			2d	• know there are different kinds of responsibilities and rights at home/school/community, and that these can sometimes conflict with each other
			2e	• reflect on moral, social and cultural issues, using imagination to understand other people's experiences
			2f	• resolve differences by looking at alternatives, making decisions and explaining choices
			4a	• know that their actions affect themselves and others, to care about other people's feelings and to try to see things from their points of view
			4c	• develop skills to be effective in relationships
			4d	• realise the nature and consequences of racism, teasing, bullying and aggressive behaviours, and how to respond to them and ask for help
			4e	• recognise and challenge stereotypes
			4g	• know where individuals can get help and support
Northern Ireland*	KS 2 (Y4/5)	Personal Development	Personal Understanding and Health	• investigate their personal self image, self-esteem and feelings and emotions
			Mutual Understanding in the Local and Wider Community	• know how to recognise, manage and express their feelings and emotions
				• recognise and be sensitive to the feelings of others
				• know when it is important to express their feelings to others and how to do this in a positive way
				• investigate situations they and others have faced and how this made them feel
				• recognise bullying, its effects and how it might feel to be in someone else's shoes
				• recognise real friendship, how to respond to bullying and how to support peers in a positive way
				• know ways in which conflict and suffering can be caused by words/gestures/symbols/actions and ways in which conflicts can be avoided/lessened/resolved
				• know how to be confident and express their views in unfamiliar circumstances
				• realise the consequences of anti-social behaviour
Republic of Ireland	3rd/4th Class	SPHE	Myself	• realise that each person has a unique contribution to make to various groups, situations and friendships
				• begin to develop strategies to cope with various worries or difficulties that he or she may encounter
				• talk about and reflect on a wide variety of feelings and emotions and the various situations where these may be experienced and how they may be expressed
				• identify strong feelings and learn how to express and cope with these feelings in a socially appropriate manner
				• explore how feelings can influence one's life
				• become aware of and think about choices and decisions that they make every day
				• recognise and explore the consequences of making a particular decision
				• learn and begin to devise a simple decision-making strategy
				• recognise and explore how the views, opinions, expectations and responses of others can influence personal decisions or actions
				• make individual and group decisions
			Myself and Others	• identify the behaviour that is important for harmony in families
				• appreciate the need for and the importance of friendship and interacting with others
				• explore the different aspects/types of friendship
				• begin to cope with disharmony in friendships
				• practise and recognise the importance of care and consideration, courtesy and good manners when interacting with others
				• respect and show consideration for the views,

Country	Year/Group	Subject	Curriculum Strand	Content Objectives
Republic of Ireland cont.			Myself and Others cont.	beliefs and values of others • recognise, discuss and understand bullying • explore and examine ways of dealing with bullying • listen carefully and reflectively to others • identify reasons for conflict in different situations • identify and discuss various responses to conflict situations and decide on and practise those that are the most appropriate or acceptable
			Myself and Wider World	• be aware of the importance of mutual respect and sensitivity to different values/attitudes of others • develop and practise leadership roles and learn to work together in different group situations • discuss/explore concept of co-operating and ways this can be put into practice in an effective manner
Scotland	P4–6	Personal and Social Development	Self-Awareness	• begin to recognise a range of emotions and how they deal with them
			Self-Esteem	• demonstrate confidence to tackle situations that they find unfamiliar • approach difficulties with confidence • recognise their perception of self is affected by responses from others
			Inter-Personal Relationships	• adopt different roles within groups • demonstrate respect and tolerance towards others
			Independence and Inter-dependence	• know when it is appropriate to seek help • discuss more than one strategy for coping with or tackling problems • take increasing responsibility for their own actions
		Health	Emotional (B)	• recognise a range of feelings they, and other people, experience at different times • communicate with others through a developing vocabulary relating to emotions and feelings • recognise the value of friendships
			Emotional (C)	• use personal/interpersonal skills to relate to people • show ways of making and keeping friends • recognise how circumstances can change emotions • show ways of dealing with a range of situations, particularly those that may present risk
			Emotional (D)	• demonstrate an understanding of their emotional needs and strengths • recognise ways behaviour can influence people's relationships
			Social (B)	• show ways of getting help
Wales	KS2 (Y3/4)	PSE	Attitudes and Values	• show care and consideration for others and be sensitive towards their feelings • respect others and value uniqueness • value friends/families as a source of love/support • value and celebrate cultural difference and diversity • take increasing responsibility for their actions • feel positive about themselves and confident in their own values
			Skills	• listen carefully/question/respond to others • empathise with others' experiences and feelings • make and maintain friendships • develop strategies to resolve conflict and deal with bullying • develop decision-making skills • work cooperatively to tackle problems
			Knowledge and Understanding	• understand the benefits of friends and families and the challenges and issues that can arise • understand the nature of bullying and harm that can result • know and understand the range of their own and others' feelings and emotions • understand the situations which produce conflict • recognise uniqueness of individuals • understand that their actions have consequences

*The curriculum guidelines for Northern Ireland have been taken from the proposals for the revised primary curriculum (April 2002). At the time of going to print, the finalised curriculum was not available.

Peer mediation agreement form

Date of mediation _____

Place of mediation _____

Children involved in conflict _____

_____

Mediator _____

Description of conflict _____

_____

_____

_____

_____

Solution agreed to _____

_____

_____

_____

_____

_____

_____

_____

Agreement sealed by: a handshake ☐   other ☐ _____

I agree to this solution.

signed _____ date _____

I agree to this solution.

signed _____ date _____

Mediator's signature

signed _____ date _____

Prim-Ed Publishing www.prim-ed.com

Glossary

Below are some specialised conflict resolution terms and related vocabulary used in this book. It is suggested that the meanings of these terms are consciously taught to the children to gain maximum benefit from this conflict resolution programme.

aggressive
An aggressive person acts as though their rights are more important than others. They seek to get their own way as often as possible.

assertive
An assertive person respects others and themselves equally. They feel comfortable enough to stand up for themselves and express their opinions, while still considering the needs of others.

compromise
A compromise is the settling of a problem or argument by both sides agreeing to give way a little from what each really wants.

conflict
A conflict situation may be caused by an event or a difference in two or more people's ideas/opinions. This causes unhappiness and disagreement.

empathy
To feel sympathetic towards another person.

'I' statements
'I' statements tell the way someone feels about a situation, using the word 'I' at the beginning of the statement; e.g. 'I don't like it when you call me names', 'I feel angry when you are always late.' 'I' statements should be used in the negotiation stage of conflict resolution. They are preferable to a person beginning a sentence with 'You ...' because this implicitly accuses the other person of causing the problem and decreases the chance of resolution. ('I' statements are also called "'I' messages" in some schools and publications.)

lose-lose
A conflict resolution result in which neither person achieves his or her wants and needs.

mediation
A process where a neutral third party listens to all sides to try and resolve a conflict.

mediator
A neutral third party who is called in to help two people in conflict solve the problem themselves.

negative feeling
A negative feeling is a 'bad' feeling, when a person feels unhappy.

negotiate
When people work or talk together to try to achieve an agreement to end conflict.

negotiating table
A quiet area set aside for students to solve conflict.

positive feeling
A positive feeling is a 'good' feeling, when a person feels happy.

passive
A passive person acts as though the rights of others are more important than their own. They may not feel confident enough to say how they feel.

prejudice
When people judge another by what they see or hear about a person, rather than what the person is really like.

tolerance
A tolerant person tries to understand and appreciate difference. Tolerance is a skill which can reduce conflict.

win-lose
A conflict resolution result in which one person achieves his or her wants and needs but the other person does not.

win-win
A conflict resolution result in which both people at least partially achieve their wants and needs.

Note: several other conflict resolution terms are used in the teachers notes. It is suggested these words be only used in discussion with more able children, to expand their vocabulary and understanding. These words include:

discrimination	gender
impartial	justice
multicultural	physical reaction
retaliation	stereotype
verbal reaction	

Understanding conflict – What is conflict?

Activity objectives

- Understands the meaning of conflict.
- Understands how people react to conflict.

Curriculum links

England	PSHE	• 2d know there are different kinds of responsibilities and rights at home/school/community, and that these can sometimes conflict with each other • 2f resolve differences by looking at alternatives, making decisions and explaining choices
Northern Ireland	PD	• know ways in which conflict and suffering can be caused by words/gestures/symbols/actions and ways in which conflicts can be avoided/lessened/resolved
Republic of Ireland	SPHE	• identify reasons for conflict in different situations • identify and discuss various responses to conflict situations and decide on and practise those that are the most appropriate or acceptable
Scotland	PSD	• discuss more than one strategy for coping with or tackling problems
Wales	PSE	• understand the situations which produce conflict • develop strategies to resolve conflict

Teacher information

Conflict between individuals and groups is a part of everyday life. Causes of conflict include limited resources, different needs, values or beliefs, and prejudice. Common justifications people give for becoming involved in conflict include justice, retaliation, defence or maintaining an image.

After students have completed the activity on the following page, the answers should be discussed, particularly the solutions devised by students for Question 4.

Discussion points

- What are some common causes of conflict?
- How do you feel when you are involved in a conflict?
- Is there more than one good way to solve a conflict?

Additional notes

Prim-Ed Publishing www.prim-ed.com

Read the newspaper article below.

Unfair for Fairies?

All is not well in Fairyland—it's too noisy! For the past few weeks, fairy shop owner Crystal James claims the children's parties she holds are being ruined by the new owner of the clothing shop next door, Rex Latto.

'The music he plays is so loud you can hear it in my shop,' complained Miss James. 'The children at the parties can't hear what I'm saying. Fairyland is supposed to be a quiet, gentle place, not somewhere you have to cover your ears.'

Miss James said she has asked Mr Latto to turn down the music, but he refused.

'My customers like the music I play,' he says. 'It's good for business.'

Miss James says the noise is making her lose customers and she is planning to do something about it.

1 Describe what has caused the conflict between Miss James and Mr Latto.

_____

_____

2 Write words to describe how you think both people feel about the conflict.

Miss James

Mr Latto

3 How do you feel about what is happening?

_____

_____

> **Think about what they both want.**

4 How do you think this conflict should be resolved? Give reasons.

Understanding conflict – What makes conflict worse?

Activity objective

- Identifies how physical and verbal reactions can affect conflict.

Curriculum links

England	PSHE	• 2d know there are different kinds of responsibilities and rights at home/school/community, and that these can sometimes conflict with each other • 2f resolve differences by looking at alternatives, making decisions and explaining choices
Northern Ireland	PD	• know ways in which conflict and suffering can be caused by words/gestures/symbols/actions and ways in which conflicts can be avoided/lessened/resolved
Republic of Ireland	SPHE	• identify reasons for conflict in different situations • identify and discuss various responses to conflict situations and decide on and practise those that are the most appropriate or acceptable
Scotland	PSD	• discuss more than one strategy for coping with or tackling problems
Wales	PSE	• understand the situations which produce conflict • develop strategies to resolve conflict

Teacher information

People involved in conflict often escalate it through verbal reactions (e.g. teasing, name-calling, swearing), or physical reactions (e.g. shoving, hitting, stamping feet). In this activity, students reflect on the behaviour of two people involved in a conflict and consider how different reactions can change the outcome of the conflict.

Discussion points

- What kinds of things can people say to make conflict worse? What kinds of things can they do?
- Which type of behaviour is worse?
- Why should we try to avoid making conflict worse?
- How could conflict be a positive experience?

Additional notes

What makes conflict worse?

Conflict doesn't have to be a bad experience. It can bring about change or new opportunities if dealt with properly. But people often make conflict worse by doing things that make others feel angry. This can be done with words (e.g. name-calling or teasing) or actions (e.g. pushing, kicking).

① Imagine you are the director of this unfinished movie scene.

> Jack and Sam are brothers who have both saved some money. They have enough between them to buy a computer game, but they are arguing over which game they should get. While they are arguing, Sam pushes Jack.

② Freeze the action! Think about what Sam might do next if Jack:

(a) *kicks him.* _____

(b) *calls him names.* _____

(c) *runs away.* _____

(d) *steps back and speaks calmly.* _____

_____

③ Which of these do you think would make the conflict worse? _____

④ You want the scene to end with the boys agreeing to a decision.
What will you tell the actor playing Jack to do when Sam pushes him? Why?

_____

_____

_____

_____

_____

_____

_____

What was your attitude?

⑤ Write one thing you have done to make a conflict worse, and what you could have done instead.

_____

_____

_____

_____

_____

_____

_____

_____

_____

_____

_____

Understanding conflict – Prejudice

Activity objectives

- Gains an understanding of prejudice.
- Understands how prejudice can cause conflict.

Curriculum links

England	PSHE	• 4e recognise and challenge stereotypes
Northern Ireland	PD	• know ways in which conflict and suffering can be caused by words/gestures/symbols/actions and ways in which conflicts can be avoided/lessened/resolved
Republic of Ireland	SPHE	• identify reasons for conflict in different situations
Scotland	PSD	• demonstrate respect and tolerance towards others
Wales	PSE	• respect others and value uniqueness

Teacher information

It is common to base initial judgments of people on stereotypes. Stereotypes depend on conventional ideas about groups of people, which may include attitudes, interests, characteristic traits or physical features.

We all stereotype people to some extent. However, stereotyping can lead to discrimination and intolerance.

After completing the activity on the following page, teachers may like students to compare their answers in small groups, and perhaps report to the class.

Discussion points

- What is prejudice?
- Why should we avoid prejudice?
- Why do you think people have prejudiced ideas?
- Discuss groups of people that are commonly stereotyped.
- Discuss other examples of how prejudice against others can lead to conflict.

Additional notes

Prejudice

Sometimes conflict begins because of prejudice.

Prejudice means that you judge a person by things you can see (e.g. age, gender or clothes) or what others have told you about him/her, rather than what the person is like.

1 Write a prejudiced idea someone might have about these people at first sight.

All elderly people are _____

_____

All people who wear glasses are _____

_____

Are these statements true for all people? Yes   No

2 **Write how each of these prejudiced ideas might cause conflict.**

(a) A brother says to his sister: 'You do the dishes. Girls are better at cleaning'.

_____

_____

_____

_____

(b) A child says loudly to her friend, 'The new kid is rich, so he'll be stuck-up'.

_____

_____

_____

Imagine what it feels like to be treated like this.

(c) One child says to another child she has just met, 'I don't want to talk to you. I've heard that you always lie'.

_____

_____

_____

3 What is wrong with having prejudiced ideas?

_____

_____

_____

_____

_____

_____

_____

Communication and feelings – Identifying feelings

- Shows an understanding of how people feel during conflict.
- Identifies how people show feelings through words and actions.

Curriculum links

England	PSHE	• 4a know that their actions affect themselves and others, to care about other people's feelings and to try to see things from their points of view
Northern Ireland	PD	• investigate situations they and others have faced and how this made them feel
Republic of Ireland	SPHE	• talk about and reflect on a wide variety of feelings and emotions and the various situations where these may be experienced and how they may be expressed
Scotland	Health	• recognise a range of feelings they, and other people, experience at different times
Wales	PSE	• empathise with others' experiences and feelings

Teacher information

Students should be able to identify common feelings of people involved in conflict. These may include positive and negative feelings; e.g. anger, disappointment, fear, frustration; confidence, calmness.

Ask the students to find partners to work with, then cut out and distribute one copy of the scenarios below to each pair. The students will need to give names to their characters.

Each scenario has a different type of ending: 'What's on TV?' has a 'win-win' ending; 'The picture book' has a 'win-lose' ending and 'Tug of war' has a 'lose-lose' ending. Teachers may like to discuss these terms with the class (refer to the glossary on page xi) and explore the feelings the characters have at the end of each role-play.

Encourage the students to use well-structured arguments in their role-plays, as well as gesture, facial expression and vocal expression to indicate their characters' feelings.

Students may perform for the whole class or a small group.

Discussion points

- What are some common feelings people involved in conflict have?
- How do they show these feelings?

What's on TV?

A and B are sisters or brothers.

They both want to watch their favourite television shows, which are about to start at the same time on different channels. They start to argue about who gets to watch his/her show.

A eventually volunteers to videotape his/her show. A and B agree that A can watch the tape whenever he/she likes. When the shows are on next week, B will tape his/her show. They shake hands.

The picture book

A and B are in the same class at school.

They are designing and writing a picture book together for a competition their teacher has entered them in.

A and B start to discuss the picture book, and realise they each have very different ideas. A tells B his/her ideas are stupid. A says he/she will only cooperate if his/her ideas are used. B backs down and unhappily agrees.

Tug of war

A and B are shoppers.

They have both picked up an item on sale. A has one end of the item and B has the other. It is the last item of its kind left. They begin to argue over who should have it, then begin a tug of war with the item. It breaks.

Identifying feelings

1. Read each scenario, then complete the following tasks with your partner.

   (a) Decide who will play A and B in each scenario.

   (b) For each one, list the feelings you think the characters might have, in order, from the beginning of the scenario to the end.

The picture book

A

B

What's on TV?

A

B

Tug of war

A

B

2. Practise your three role-plays. Make sure you say at least four lines each. Choose your words and actions carefully to show how your character is feeling.

3. Perform your role-plays for the class or a small group.

4. On your own, choose one of the role-plays you performed. Describe how you showed your character's feelings.

Title of role-play _____ Character ☐ A ☐ B

_____

_____

_____

_____

Communication and feelings – How would you feel?

Activity objectives

- Understands the difference between positive and negative feelings.
- Considers how some conflict situations might make him/her feel.
- Considers how some conflict situations might make others feel.

Curriculum links

England	PSHE	• 4a know that their actions affect themselves and others, to care about other people's feelings and to try to see things from their points of view • 2f resolve differences by looking at alternatives, making decisions and explaining choices
Northern Ireland	PD	• investigate situations they and others have faced and how this made them feel • know ways in which conflict and suffering can be caused by words/gestures/symbols/actions and ways in which conflicts can be avoided/lessened/resolved
Republic of Ireland	SPHE	• talk about and reflect on a wide variety of feelings and emotions and the various situations where these may be experienced and how they may be expressed • identify and discuss various responses to conflict situations and decide on and practise those that are the most appropriate or acceptable
Scotland	Health PSD	• recognise a range of feelings they, and other people, experience at different times • discuss more than one strategy for coping with or tackling problems
Wales	PSE	• empathise with others' experiences and feelings • develop strategies to resolve conflict

Teacher information

Most people associate conflict with negative thoughts or feelings such as unhappiness, anger and violence, but if dealt with correctly, conflict can also be a positive experience, motivating change and providing opportunities.

Our families, cultures, schools, workplaces and communities teach us different ways to deal with conflict, but it is commonly accepted that one side wins and the other loses. However, students should be encouraged to strive for a 'win-win' outcome to conflict. This concept is covered in the pages concerned with conflict resolution.

After the activity is completed, teachers may like to hold a class discussion about appropriate and inappropriate ways to express feelings.

Students could compare their answers with a partner when they have finished.

Discussion points

- What is a common way to express anger/fear/frustration/sadness/happiness etc.?
- What effect can feelings have on a conflict?

Additional notes

Prim-Ed Publishing www.prim-ed.com

How would you feel?

How do you feel when you are involved in conflict? Depending on how you deal with the conflict, you may have negative feelings like sadness and anger or positive feelings like pride and satisfaction.

Read the conflicts below and then answer the questions.

You and your brother are supposed to walk home from school together every day. You always have to wait for him because he talks to his friends. You and he constantly argue on the way home about this. He says he will take as long as he likes. You say it is unfair for you to have to wait for him.

1 Write words to describe how this conflict would make you feel.

_____

_____

_____

2 Write words to describe how this conflict would make your brother feel.

_____

_____

_____

3 Tick any positive feelings and cross any negative feelings you wrote.

4 How could you resolve the conflict so both of you felt positively about it?

_____

_____

_____

_____

You borrowed your best friend's favourite book. You left it lying around one day, and your dog chewed it. When you gave it back to your friend, he/she called you horrible names. You apologised, but your friend refused to accept your apology.

1 Write words to describe how this conflict would make you feel.

_____

_____

_____

2 Write words to describe how this conflict would make your friend feel.

_____

_____

_____

3 Tick any positive feelings and cross any negative feelings you wrote.

4 How could you resolve the conflict so that both of you felt positively about it?

_____

_____

_____

Communication and feelings – Responses to conflict

Activity objective

- Evaluates how he/she responds to conflict.

Curriculum links

England	PSHE	• 2f resolve differences by looking at alternatives, making decisions and explaining choices
Northern Ireland	PD	• know ways in which conflict and suffering can be caused by words/gestures/symbols/actions and ways in which conflicts can be avoided/lessened/resolved
Republic of Ireland	SPHE	• identify and discuss various responses to conflict situations and decide on and practise those that are the most appropriate or acceptable
Scotland	PSD	• discuss more than one strategy for coping with or tackling problems
Wales	PSE	• develop strategies to resolve conflict

Teacher information

The following page can be completed as a class exercise or given to individual students after a conflict has taken place.

Discussion points

- Describe how you usually respond to conflict.
- How could you improve on your usual response to conflict?
- What did you learn from the last conflict you were involved in?

Additional notes

Responses to conflict

How do you usually respond to conflict? Answer these questions.

1 What type of conflict were you last involved in (e.g. an argument, bullying)?

_____

2 How many others were involved? _____

3 Tick the box or boxes that describe what you did.

(a) When the conflict began:

I ignored it. ☐

I responded after a while. ☐

I responded immediately. ☐

Other _____

_____

_____

(b) During the conflict:

I used violent words or actions. ☐

I used non-violent words or actions. ☐

Describe _____

_____

4 Tick the box or boxes that show the result of the conflict.

People were hurt. ☐   Describe _____

_____

We agreed to disagree. ☐   Describe _____

_____

We resolved the conflict. ☐   Describe _____

_____

We asked someone else to help us. ☐   Describe _____

_____

Communication and feelings – Being a good listener

Activity objectives

- Identifies the importance of active listening.
- Identifies the steps necessary to become an active listener.

Curriculum links

England	PSHE	• 4c develop skills to be effective in relationships
Northern Ireland	PD	• know ways in which conflict and suffering can be caused and ways in which conflicts can be avoided
Republic of Ireland	SPHE	• listen carefully and reflectively to others
Scotland	Health	• use personal/interpersonal skills to relate to people
Wales	PSE	• listen carefully/question/respond to others

Teacher information

Many people fail to interpret correctly what other people are saying for a number of reasons. They may be preparing their own responses, the speaker may not have the attention of the audience, so their focus may wander to other things, or those listening may feel the need to say something and therefore interrupt rather than letting the other person finish first.

Listening is a skill vital in all areas of learning. It may be learnt and developed in a number of ways. Listening to audio tapes and stories, following directions, listening to instructions and repeating messages are some activities which help to develop communication skills.

Listening to and respecting another person's point of view is an important skill used to prevent and resolve conflicts.

How to be a good listener.

- Look at the speaker.
- Listen without interrupting.
- Concentrate on what the speaker is saying.
- Ask questions to find out more.
- Show that you understand by nodding, making eye contact and using facial expressions.
- Repeat what you have heard in your own words. (This is perhaps the most important.)

Discussion points

- Why is it important to be a good listener?
- What can happen if you don't listen to someone properly?
- Are you sure that you know what someone else is saying?

Additional activities

- Students construct a sociogram detailing those people they could go to with any problems or concerns.
- To complete this activity the students will need to listen to a short talk by another member of the class. The students may be given five minutes to think of as much information as possible on a given subject; for example, their favourite author, sports team, sportsman, TV show, TV star or singer. At the completion of each talk, a member of the audience is asked to repeat the talk in his/her own words, including as much information as was given. (Students can record the information on a sheet of paper.)

Being a good listener

① What class rules are necessary to ensure good listening? Why are they necessary?

_____

_____

_____

_____

② Think of a friend, neighbour or family member who always listens to what you have to say.

Draw him/her.

③ What qualities make a person a good listener?

_____

_____

_____

_____

④ If you had to tell someone how to listen properly, how would you tell him/her to do it? Write five steps for teaching someone how to listen well.

1

2

3

4

5

Communication and feelings – Communication skills

Activity objectives

- Identifies different types of communication.
- Changes statements to vary communication.

Curriculum links

England	PSHE	• 4c develop skills to be effective in relationships
Northern Ireland	PD	• know when it is important to express feelings to others and how to do this in a positive way
Republic of Ireland	SPHE	• identify strong feelings and learn how to express and cope with these feelings in a socially appropriate manner
Scotland	Health	• use personal/interpersonal skills to relate to people
Wales	PSE	• feel positive about themselves and confident in their own values

Teacher information

People communicate in a variety of ways. Verbal and nonverbal methods of communication include facial expressions, body language, tone and volume of voice. Communication can take three styles: passive, aggressive or assertive.

Passive people act as though the rights of others are more important than theirs. They may feel inclined to act in a particular way and not feel confident enough to say how they feel or what they would prefer to do.

Aggressive people act as though their rights are more important than others. They try to get their own way as much as possible, using bullying or physical violence.

Assertive people respect others and themselves equally. They feel confident enough to stand up for themselves and to express their opinions, while considering the needs of others.

Ideally, students will learn to use strategies such as 'self-talk', including 'I' statements and repeating self-affirming statements. These could include, 'I am special', 'I deserve to be treated with respect' and 'I know the things being said about me aren't true'. Completing 'I' statements allows students to indicate what happened, how they felt, why they felt that way and what they would like to happen instead. For example:

- 'When Callum pinched me, I didn't like it because it hurt, so I would like him to stop doing it.'

- 'When Abbey wouldn't play with me, I felt sad because I like her and would like to be her friend, so I would like her to let me play with her sometimes.'

Discussion points

- What do the words 'aggressive', 'passive' and 'assertive' mean? Look them up in a dictionary and discuss the various definitions found.
- Discuss the characteristics of 'aggressive', 'passive' and 'assertive' people.
- Can a person be passive and assertive, depending on the situation? For example; a student may be passive at school, but assertive at home with family members. Another student may be very aggressive and assertive on the sports field but passive in the classroom.
- Explain that it is possible for people to practise changing the way they speak ('I' statements) and act (body language), training themselves to be more assertive or less aggressive.
- Show a range of pictures. Discuss whether the person feels good or bad about himself/ herself. Students can role-play how they look, act and speak when they are feeling good or bad about themselves.

Additional notes

1 There are three main types of communication – assertive, passive and aggressive. Look at the pictures below. Write the type of communication used in each situation.

_____   _____

2 Change these passive statements to assertive statements.

- *'Okay, I'll let you in front of me in the line.'*

_____

- *'I know my jeans don't have a label.'*

_____

- *'I don't know if this is my pencil or not.'*

_____

- *'All right, I'll give it to you.'*

_____

3 Change these aggressive statements to assertive statements.

- *'It's not yours! It's mine!'*

_____

- *'Get your own paper!'*

_____

- *'Go away! We don't want you to play!'*

_____

4 I think I am an/a _____ communicator.

(passive/aggressive/assertive)

tell yourself you are all right   take deep breaths   consider the best way to react

Communication and feelings – Communication activities

Activity objective

- Communicates in a variety of ways.

Curriculum links

England	PSHE	• 4c develop skills to be effective in relationships
Northern Ireland	PD	• recognise real friendship and how to support peers in a positive way
Republic of Ireland	SPHE	• appreciate the need for and the importance of friendship and interacting with others
Scotland	Health	• recognise the value of friendships
Wales	PSE	• value friends/families as a source of love/support

Teacher information

Being able to communicate effectively enables students to feel that they are getting their point across. Communication may take many forms. The same point of view or opinion may be expressed in a number of creative ways. Students may feel more confident to express their feelings through poetry, artwork, drama, mime or creative writing.

Games such as 'Shapes' and 'Sculptures', where students form groups of three to create a shape as directed by the teacher, use body language to communicate ideas. Activities such as debates, short talks, role-plays, singing, reciting raps or poetry, allowing students to lead displays or assembly items, or assisting younger children, are only a few ways to develop confidence and communication skills. Most students have talents in one or two particular areas and would prefer to communicate using these methods. It is advisable to give the students opportunities to develop and experience skills and activities in a variety of communication methods.

The activities on page 19 allow the students to use a variety of creative methods to communicate the same thoughts.

Discussion points

- What is your most commonly used method of communication?
- If you wanted to share your thoughts or feelings with someone, who would you choose and how would you do it?
- Which 'creative' method of communication do you enjoy using the most?
- Think of a painting or play that you have seen. What do you think the artist or playwright is trying to express?
- Which ones did you like the best?
- Which creative method of communication did most people choose?
- Were there any class members who displayed a talent that you didn't know they had?

Additional notes

Communication activities

1 Read the poems below:

> Four
> Faithful
> Friends
> Frequently
> Find
> Fabulous
> Fun
> For
> Fascinating
> Foolishness

> I talk to you,
> You talk to me.
> I am your friend,
> As you can see.
> I listen to you,
> You listen to me.
> We know each other,
> Communication is the key.

2 Complete a poem about what your friend(s) means to you. You may choose to write any type of poem you wish.

_____

_____

_____

_____

_____

_____

_____

_____

_____

_____

_____

_____

3 Read the activities listed below and choose three to communicate the theme 'What having a close friend means to me':

- Create a friendship mask using recycled materials.
- Paint an picture using any medium that you have available.
- Make a sculpture using recycled materials and explain its meaning.
- Write a short play and perform it with some friends.
- Write a simple song and perform it for the class.
- Write a rap about your best friend, choose some music and perform it for the class.
- Create a mime and perform it with a friend.

4 Share your completed activities with the class.

Communication and feelings - 'I' statements

Activity objective

- Completes 'I' statements to respond to a specific situation.

Curriculum links

England	PSHE	• 4c develop skills to be effective in relationships
Northern Ireland	PD	• know when it is important to express their feelings to others and how to do this in a positive way
		• know how to be confident and express their views in unfamiliar circumstances
Republic of Ireland	SPHE	• identify and discuss various responses to conflict situations and decide on and practise those that are the most appropriate or acceptable
Scotland	Health	• use personal/interpersonal skills to relate to people
Wales	PSE	• develop strategies to resolve conflict

Teacher information

Being able to communicate effectively enables students to feel that they are getting their point across. One way to do this without making being aggressive is to be assertive and use 'I' statements.

'I' statements are likely to be more effective because they cannot be disputed. Students can begin sentences with 'I feel ...', or 'I don't like the way ...', so that they cannot be argued with because it is how they are feeling! Also, by expressing how he or she is feeling, the student is not making judgments about the person he/she is disagreeing with (so the person needn't become defensive!).

Three points to remember when being assertive and using 'I' statements are:
- Begin the sentence with 'I'.
- State how you feel.
- State the specific behaviour you don't like.

Students don't have to stick strictly to a formula as long as the basic structure is kept; for example, 'I'm starting to get angry', 'I don't like being called names' and 'I didn't realise this is so important to you, can we work this out?'

Teaching problem-solving strategies through discussion and role-playing will assist students to learn and develop skills for positive social behaviours and relationships. 'I' statements are a good example of this. It is also important that the students making the 'I' statement have the body language to match.

Discussion points

- What are some words to describe how you are feeling? Make a list of words for reference; for example, embarrassed, hurt, angry, confused, upset.
- Allow the students to share their responses to Question 2. Many different responses may be appropriate.
- Do not force students to respond to a very personal situation in front of others if they do not feel comfortable doing so.
- Role-play a conversation or argument that is full of 'you' statements. Ask the class to help change the dialogue to 'I' statements.
- Discuss situations which evoke certain feelings. Students tell situations where they felt embarrassed, upset, uncomfortable, angry, sad etc.

Additional notes

Conflict Resolution

Prim-Ed Publishing www.prim-ed.com

1 Look at the picture and answer the questions.

> Where did you get the shirt? From a jumble sale?

> My mum made it. I think it's great, because my mum is really clever and she let me choose my own pattern and material. It's one of a kind!

Is this an appropriate response to the situation? Yes No

Is it a good 'I' statement? Yes No *Why?* _____

_____

_____

2 Write 'I' statements in response to the following situations. Use this formula:

'I' feel (state the feeling) ... when you (describe the other person's behaviour)... because ... (describe how the person's behaviour is affecting you).

(a) A girl in your class spreads some rumours about you. _____

_____

_____

(b) One of your friends won't let you join in the game. _____

_____

(c) When you go to play on your usual climbing frame in the playground at lunchtime, some other boys are playing there already.

_____

_____

(d) You need to use a specific felt-tipped pen to complete your work. You think the girl next to you has yours.

_____

_____

Communication and feelings – What makes you angry?

Activity objectives

- Identifies situations that may cause anger.
- Identifies strategies for controlling anger.

Curriculum links

England	PSHE	• 4c develop skills to be effective in relationships
Northern Ireland	PD	• know how to recognise, manage and express their feelings and emotions
Republic of Ireland	SPHE	• identify strong feelings and learn how to express and cope with these feelings in a socially appropriate manner
Scotland	PSD	• begin to recognise a range of emotions and how they deal with them
Wales	PSE	• know and understand the range of their own and others' feelings and emotions

Teacher information

All students will experience anger in one situation or another. They should be aware that anger is a normal reaction to certain situations. It is how they react when they are angry that causes conflicts to escalate. Students may become angry for the following reasons:

- conflict–verbal or physical,
- rejection–not being allowed to play with their friends etc.,
- being asked or made to do things they don't want to do,
- having their property or space invaded.

Students should feel comfortable enough in the classroom to express and learn to manage feelings of anger.

Teachers should be able to provide simple strategies to help students to deal with anger in a socially acceptable manner.

Some acceptable ways of controlling anger include:

- taking deep breaths,
- counting to 10,
- getting away from the situation or person that is making you angry,
- trying to relax your body,
- exercising–going for a walk or bouncing a ball etc.,
- trying to stay calm;
- thinking and choosing the best way to react,
- telling yourself you are all right,
- talking about how you feel.

Discussion points

- Brainstorm situations where students feel anger and list these on the board.
- Is it all right to be angry? When? Why?/Why not?
- What things shouldn't you do when you are angry?
- Is it all right to hurt someone's feelings when you are angry?
- How does being angry make you feel? What do you look like? What do you do? What things are all right to do when you are angry?
- Have you ever regretted something you have done when you've been angry?
- What are some things you could do to control anger?

Additional notes

What makes you angry?

1. In the spaces provided, write some situations when you feel angry.

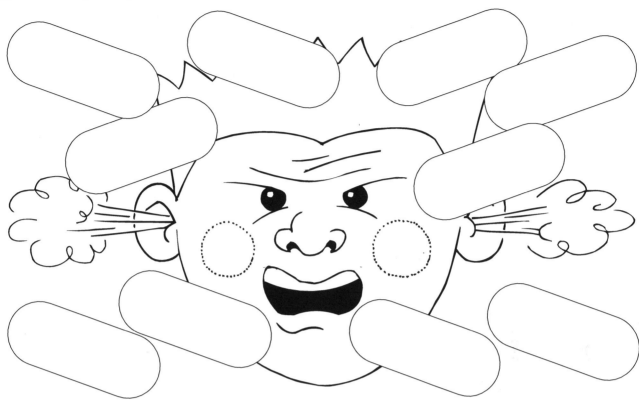

2. It is okay to feel angry. It is what you do when you are angry that can be a problem.

Suitable Reactions	Unsuitable Reactions

3. Write three simple steps that you could take to control your anger.

_____

_____

_____

Communication and feelings – Human rights

Activity objectives

- Identifies rights and responsibilities.
- Devises a list of rights and responsibilities.

Curriculum links

England	PSHE	• 2d know there are different kinds of responsibilities and rights at home/school/community, and that these can sometimes conflict with each other
Northern Ireland	PD	• know ways in which conflict and suffering can be caused by words/gestures/symbols/actions and ways in which conflicts can be avoided/lessened/resolved
Republic of Ireland	SPHE	• identify reasons for conflict in different situations • identify and discuss various responses to conflict situations and decide on and practise those that are the most appropriate or acceptable
Scotland	PSD	• demonstrate respect and tolerance towards others
Wales	PSE	• understand the situations which produce conflict

Teacher information

Teaching children tolerance is also teaching them not to hate. It is the beginning of respecting the rights of others. Children should be taught to appreciate and respect differences in others. As a role model, it is every teacher's responsibility to display tolerant behaviour in the classroom and playground.

The international global community has decided on basic human rights which are called the General Declaration of Human Rights. The list includes:

- Right to human dignity
- Right to privacy
- Right to private property
- Equality before the law
- Freedom of movement
- Freedom of thought, conscience and religion
- Right to education
- Right to personal freedom

This list has been formulated in an effort to ensure countries and their people support the basic rights and freedom of all.

Students have the right to feel safe when they are at school. They also have the right to be treated with respect and kindness; express their feelings and opinions; and work and play in an environment that has consistent, fair rules.

Students have a responsibility to respect the rights of others.

Discussion points

- What does 'right' mean?
- What is the meaning of 'responsibility'?
- What is the difference between 'rights' and 'responsibilities'?
- What are some rights and responsibilities you have at home?
- Have there been times when you have been denied your rights at home? When? Why?
- Have there been any times when you have not fulfilled your responsibilities at home? When? Why? What happened?
- What are some rights and responsibilities that you have at school?
- Do people in other countries have the same rights as we do? Why/Why not?

Additional notes

Prim-Ed Publishing www.prim-ed.com

Human rights

1 Look at the list below. Circle the rights and underline the responsibilities.

education   *clean food*   *clean water*   *play safely*   *respect others*   *privacy*

do my best   *safety*   *obey the rules*   *freedom from harm*

2 List some rights and responsibilities you have at home.

Rights

Responsibilities

3 What do you think happens when rights are not respected?

_____

_____

_____

4 Can you think of any countries where human rights may not be respected?

You are unique. No one is the same as you. People deserve to be accepted as they are.

Communication and feelings – Empathy

Activity objectives

- Considers the meaning of empathy.
- Expresses the points of view of others.

Curriculum links

England	PSHE	• 4a know that their actions affect themselves and others, to care about other people's feelings and to try to see things from their points of view
Northern Ireland	PD	• recognise and be sensitive to the feelings of others
Republic of Ireland	SPHE	• practise and recognise the importance of care and consideration, courtesy and good manners when interacting with others
Scotland	Health	• recognise a range of feelings they, and other people, experience at different times
Wales	PSE	• empathise with others' experiences and feelings

Teacher information

Empathy means 'mentally entering into the feeling or spirit of a person or thing'. Simply speaking, 'empathy' means to feel sympathetic towards another person or to be in accord with him/her. For children this means putting themselves in someone else's place and imagining how that person feels. Students need to be appreciative and tolerant of differences in others. It is sometimes easier for students to ridicule the unknown or unfamiliar than show sympathy and understanding. This activity will help students to put themselves in the place of another person.

Students will need access to a dictionary to complete this activity.

The poem 'Feelings' may be used as an introduction to this topic.

Feelings

When I feel sad and want to cry,
My face screws up and boo hoo hoo
I need to know it's what people do
And my friends have feelings too
If I get mad and in a stew
I stamp my feet and my face turns blue
I need to remember it's what we all do
And my friends often feel that way too.
Sometimes I'm scared 'cause someone said 'BOO!!'
Or I'm frightened to do something new
I remind myself it's what we all do
And my friends have feelings too
I like being happy and laugh when I do
It's the best feeling to have, especially with you
And it's nice to remember feeling is what we all do
And my friends have feelings too.

Discussion points

- What does 'empathy' mean? Is this the same as sympathy?
- Is it okay to feel sorry for someone?
- How do you feel when you hear a sad or tragic news item? Do you think about how those people or their families are feeling?
- Can you think of a news item that you saw that made you feel sad for the people in the story?

Additional notes

Empathy

① Look up the word 'empathy' in the dictionary.

Write the meaning here. _____

_____

_____

② Read the examples below. In the space provided say how you think you would feel in the same situation.

Stephanie is going on a camping holiday and her parents say that it is okay for Georgia to go as well, as long as her parents agree. Georgia has never been away without her parents before.

Bryson has to walk home alone from football training every Wednesday afternoon. Along the way, he has to pass a house where a vicious dog lives. Today, as he walks towards the house, he can see that the gate is open.

Jayden has just moved to a new house. It is his first day at a new school. He doesn't know anyone in his class and he hasn't had time to meet any other children in the neighbourhood.

Tiffany is a quiet child in the class. She always seems to sit by herself. She is the youngest in her family and has five brothers and sisters. Her clothes are usually hand-me-downs and she brings her school things in a plastic bag.

③ Write the word 'empathy' down the side of a sheet of paper and write an acrostic poem. Illustrate your poem appropriately to show that you understand its meaning.

Team building – What makes a good team?

Activity objective

- Gains an understanding of the qualities of a good team.

Curriculum links

England	PSHE	• 4c develop skills to be effective in relationships
Northern Ireland	PD	• recognise real friendship and how to support peers in a positive way
Republic of Ireland	SPHE	• develop and practise leadership roles and learn to work together in different group situations
		• discuss/explore concept of co-operating and ways this can be put into practice in an effective manner
Scotland	Health	• use personal/interpersonal skills to relate to people
Wales	PSE	• work cooperatively to tackle problems

Teacher information

Students could describe teams they have belonged to; e.g. school, sport, at home, in the community, for competitions. Some team-building activities are provided on page 33.

After they complete the activity on the following page, teachers might like to hold a class discussion on the qualities of a good team.

The qualities of a good team include:

Working towards a clear goal – the team clearly understands and works towards the goal that is to be achieved. Each team member is focused on the tasks he/she is allocated by the team. The team may define any targets that need to be achieved as it works towards the goal.

Good communication – the team members listen to each other with respect and willingly share their ideas without domination. Through this, the team members develop a mutual trust. Logical decisions are made with the acceptance of all team members.

Consideration – the team members encourage and support each other's ideas, giving critical feedback. Any criticism is aimed at the idea, rather than the person who contributed the idea. This encourages a willingness for the team to take risks and create new ideas. Everyone has an important role in the team.

Discussion points

- What teams are you/have you been a member of?
- What qualities or skills does a good team member have?
- What could an effective team achieve compared to an ineffective one?
- When do people work in teams?

Additional notes

Conflict Resolution

Prim-Ed Publishing www.prim-ed.com

What makes a good team?

1 Read this diary entry.

Dear Diary

It's strange being at a new school but everyone's really friendly. I want to play in the basketball team, so I spoke to the coach yesterday. He invited me to watch the team play.

I knew the school had an excellent basketball team, and I soon saw why. Before the game started, the coach asked the team members to tell him the goal of playing. Everyone knew what it was—to try hard while playing fairly. Next, they talked about their strategies. I noticed the team members listened to each other without interrupting. If someone didn't like an idea, he/she criticised the idea, not the person who thought of it.

During the game, the team was focused on its goal—everyone was doing his or her best. The players were also supportive of each other. If someone scored a goal, the team clapped and cheered. If someone missed, the team called out encouraging words. This motivated people to take risks, trying some difficult moves—which often paid off.

At half-time, our team was two goals down. With the coach's help, the team members made some decisions on what they could do to improve their playing. They made sure everyone agreed before they finished talking.

During the last half, the team was on fire! I was so excited when they won. I can't wait to become a part of this team.

Ben

2

List the qualities of a good team that Ben saw. Compare your answers to a partner's.

_____

_____

_____

_____

_____

_____

_____

_____

Team building – Teamwork evaluation

Activity objectives

- Evaluates the effectiveness of a team he/she has been part of.
- Evaluates the effectiveness of himself/herself as a team member.

Curriculum links

England	PSHE	• 4c develop skills to be effective in relationships
Northern Ireland	PD	• recognise real friendship and how to support peers in a positive way
Republic of Ireland	SPHE	• develop and practise leadership roles and learn to work together in different group situations
		• discuss/explore concept of co-operating and ways this can be put into practice in an effective manner
Scotland	Health	• use personal/interpersonal skills to relate to people
	PSD	• adopt different roles within groups
Wales	PSE	• work cooperatively to tackle problems

Teacher information

These proformas are for use after students complete a team activity, which may include team games or group projects/activities in areas such as science, technology and drama.

Discussion points

- How could you become a better team member?
- What areas does the last team you were in need to work on?
- Do you think all team members should contribute? Why?

Additional notes

Teamwork group evaluation

Members of team: _____

_____

Team's goal: _____

_____

The team understood the goal. ☐ Yes ☐ No

The team worked towards the goal. ☐ Yes ☐ No

Everyone participated. ☐ Yes ☐ No

We listened to each other's ideas. ☐ Yes ☐ No

We made decisions everyone agreed to. ☐ Yes ☐ No

We solved problems together. ☐ Yes ☐ No

We encouraged each other to take risks. ☐ Yes ☐ No

We achieved the goal. ☐ Yes ☐ No

Write words to describe your team. _____

Teamwork self-evaluation

Members of team: _____

_____

Team's goal: _____

_____

I understood the goal. ☐ Yes ☐ No

I worked towards the goal. ☐ Yes ☐ No

I contributed some great ideas. ☐ Yes ☐ No

I listened to others. ☐ Yes ☐ No

I took part in making decisions. ☐ Yes ☐ No

I took risks. ☐ Yes ☐ No

Write words to describe what kind of team member you were.

Team building – Team building activities

Activity objective

- Participates in team building activities.

Curriculum links

England	PSHE	• 4c develop skills to be effective in relationships
Northern Ireland	PD	• recognise real friendship and how to support peers in a positive way
Republic of Ireland	SPHE	• develop and practise leadership roles and learn to work together in different group situations
		• discuss/explore concept of co-operating and ways this can be put into practice in an effective manner
Scotland	Health	• use personal/interpersonal skills to relate to people
	PSD	• adopt different roles within groups
Wales	PSE	• work cooperatively to tackle problems

Teacher information

Each of the team building activities on the following page can be given to a small group. Teachers should set a time limit for each activity.

The activities foster team skills such as communication, negotiation, working towards a goal, problem-solving, allocating tasks, risk-taking and creative thinking.

Before completing any activity, instruct the students that talking to their team members is vital to complete each task successfully. The whole team must also agree on each decision that is made before it is carried out.

Team numbers are suggested for each activity, but may be changed if teachers feel it is necessary.

As well as the materials listed below, each group will require paper and pens to write ideas and/ or plans for each activity, with the exception of 'Monsters'.

Teachers may like to have each team present its creations/ideas to the class in the case of 'Make a picture book' and 'The cheats'. 'Who, what, where?' and 'Monsters' must be presented to the class.

A class discussion and student evaluation should follow the completion of each activity.

Additional information for each activity

Make a picture book

- Each team will need thick card and/or paper which it can staple together to make an eight-page book with a front cover. Tell the students to finish the pages before stapling them together. Groups will also require writing materials.

- Teachers should read some suitable children's books to the class before the teams start work.
- Depending on the ability of the class, teachers may like to give the students a theme for their books; e.g. an animal story, a story to teach children about colours.

Who, what, where?

- Teachers will need to make cards for the class with character, object and setting words on them. Some suggestions are:

  Character professor, rock star, shop assistant, taxi driver, hairdresser, sportsperson, waiter

  Object frying pan, glass of water, spoon, book, candle, pencil, paper bag, teddy bear

  Setting doctor's waiting room, airport, train carriage, fun park, museum, park, shops

- Teachers may like to have the actual objects for students to use as props. It is suggested that the students only be allowed to use the props during their performances.

The cheats

- Encourage students to read the task carefully before they begin work. Teachers may suggest that teams nominate one person to read the problem aloud.
- Encourage teams to come up with at least three steps for catching the cheats.

Monsters

- Teachers may like to show pictures of monsters before students begin the activity.
- Teachers could change the number of legs the monsters have to make it easier/more difficult.

Discussion points

- What problems did your team encounter? How did you solve them?
- Were you happy with your team's work? Why/ Why not?

Team building activities

Make a picture book

Group of 4

Make an eight-page picture book that is suitable for a parent to read to a three-year-old. You will need to decide on:

- a simple story,
- suitable colours,
- illustrations,
- an attractive front cover.

You should decide on a story first, then discuss what the book should look like.

Who, what, where?

Group of 4

Your group should have three cards – one with a character, one with an object and one with a setting.

Your task is to plan and act out a short scene that involves these three things. Your story must have a beginning, middle and ending and every person in the group must have at least three lines to say.

You should practise and rehearse your scene, then present it to the class.

The cheats

Group of 4

You are a group of teachers. Your classes have just completed the same important test. You suspect that four of the children cheated because they have exactly the same answers.

The list of answers was in a drawer in one of your classrooms the day before the test. It is still there, but it has dirty fingerprints on it.

You want to prove these four children cheated without letting them know what you are doing. Write a list of steps you could take to get some proof. You will need to agree on each step before you write it.

Monsters

Group of 5

Make a six-legged monster with your group, with each person being a part of the monster. Your monster must be able to move and must make a sound.

Begin by deciding what your monster will look like and which part(s) each person will be.

Hints
- The monster's legs could be people's arms, legs, elbows, knees etc.
- Use your imagination! Fingers could be claws, elbows could be spines etc.
- Group members can be sitting, standing, lying, kneeling etc.

Conflict resolution skills – Conflict resolution steps

The steps on page 35 are one format for aiding

Activity objective

- Reads and discusses steps to resolve conflicts in a mutually acceptable way.

Curriculum links

England	PSHE	• 2d know there are different kinds of responsibilities and rights at home/school/community, and that these can sometimes conflict with each other • 2f resolve differences by looking at alternatives, making decisions and explaining choices
Northern Ireland	PD	• know ways in which conflict and suffering can be caused by words/gestures/symbols/actions and ways in which conflicts can be avoided/lessened/resolved
Republic of Ireland	SPHE	• identify reasons for conflict in different situations • identify and discuss various responses to conflict situations and decide on and practise those that are the most appropriate or acceptable
Scotland	PSD	• discuss more than one strategy for coping with or tackling problems
Wales	PSE	• understand the situations which produce conflict • develop strategies to resolve conflict

Teacher information

Conflict is an occurrence in every school, workplace and home. In school, it is often the case that students faced with opposing viewpoints will go to a teacher to sort out the problem and make the final decision.

Conflict resolution is a process that directs the responsibility of solving a conflict to the students. Students learn to express their point of view, voice their interests and find mutually acceptable solutions.

Conflict resolution steps are to be used, if possible, before conflicts reach a physical/violent stage. Students should be encouraged to use discussion to resolve minor conflicts such as name-calling, rumours, taking property without asking, teasing and invading personal space.

To resolve a conflict situation, students should feel comfortable enough to express their feelings, listen to others without feeling threatened and negotiate a solution that suits both parties.

The first priority is to establish a cooperative classroom and school environment where the rules, rights and responsibilities are clearly stated, and where students feel able to say what they feel. Students should be aware of class and school rules and their rights and responsibilities.

Schools that have implemented the conflict resolution programme are reporting that conflicts are being handled more quickly, physical fighting is declining and more caring behaviour is being noticed.

The steps on page 35 are one format for aiding students in resolving conflicts. The students may feel more ownership towards a set of steps if they were to make up a class set of their own. Students may wish to practise saying the exact words to help remember them and to be able to bring them to mind quickly in a heated situation.

Students may decide on a format in simple words of their own, such as the alternative below:

- What's the problem?
- How can we fix it?
- What is the best way to fix the problem?
- Choose the best option.
- Agree on the best solution and do it!

Teachers may wish to give each student a copy of the steps as a quick reference, or enlarge them and display them in the room for everyone to see.

Discussion points

- How do you usually solve minor conflicts?
- Are there different ways to resolve the same conflict?
- How can you make sure that both parties are happy with the solution?
- Have you been in any situations where you have seen (or used) conflict resolution steps to solve a problem?
- Have you seen any situations where conflict resolution steps have not been used and the conflict has escalated to physical violence?

Conflict resolution steps

1 Stop and cool off.

2 Define the problem.
(Use 'I' statements.)
- Tell the other person what happened.
- Tell the other person how you feel.

3 Brainstorm solutions.

4 Choose a solution that is fair to both of you.
(Compromise is the key!)

5 Make a plan.
Decide how you will put it into action.

6 Agree to the plan.
- A handshake is a good way to show that you agree.

Conflict resolution steps – Conflict resolution

Activity objective

- Uses conflict resolution steps to solve a problem.

Curriculum links

England	PSHE	• 2d know there are different kinds of responsibilities and rights at home/school/community, and that these can sometimes conflict with each other • 2f resolve differences by looking at alternatives, making decisions and explaining choices
Northern Ireland	PD	• know ways in which conflict and suffering can be caused by words/gestures/symbols/actions and ways in which conflicts can be avoided/lessened/resolved
Republic of Ireland	SPHE	• identify reasons for conflict in different situations • identify and discuss various responses to conflict situations and decide on and practise those that are the most appropriate or acceptable
Scotland	PSD	• discuss more than one strategy for coping with or tackling problems
Wales	PSE	• understand the situations which produce conflict • develop strategies to resolve conflict

Teacher information

Students can work in pairs to complete this activity. Teachers may wish to give a copy of the scenario to each student or group, or enlarge one copy for the class to read.

A vital step in developing appropriate conflict resolution skills involves following the steps closely and evaluating the process once a solution is reached.

Students should be able to evaluate:

- Was the solution the best?
- Was the solution fair/just?
- Were both parties happy with the solution?
- Were there other solutions that weren't considered? (Other students may suggest more creative alternatives to the conflict.)

Discussion points

- Discuss all the steps slowly and carefully with the students.
- Have you encountered a situation similar to that mentioned on page 37?
- How was the situation resolved to everyone's satisfaction?
- Were steps similar to the conflict resolution steps used to resolve the problem?
- Discuss other common situations similar to that on page 37, repeating the steps until the students are very familiar with them.

Additional notes

Conflict resolution

*Read the scenario below, then complete the conflict resolution steps to resolve the conflict.
Tick each step as you complete it.*

Sarah, Jessica and Taryn had found a flat, grassy spot in the playground. Taryn had convinced her mother to let her bring her CD player to school. Today they were going to make up a dance to go with one of their favourite songs. Sarah, who goes to jazz ballet class, thought that the last steps she had made up were the best to use in that section of the song. Jessica, who was a good gymnast, thought that the ones that she had made up were better.

① What can the girls do to cool off?

_____

_____

_____ ☐

② What is the problem?

_____

_____

_____

_____

Write an 'I' statement for each girl.

Sarah _____

_____

_____

Jessica _____

_____ ☐

③ What are some solutions to the problem?

☐

④ Which solution have you chosen?

_____

_____ ☐

⑤ How do you plan to do this?

_____

_____

_____

_____ ☐

⑥ Shake hands! Well done! ☐

Conflict resolution steps – Conflict role-plays

Curriculum links

England	PSHE	• 2d know there are different kinds of responsibilities and rights at home/school/community, and that these can sometimes conflict with each other • 2f resolve differences by looking at alternatives, making decisions and explaining choices
Northern Ireland	PD	• know ways in which conflict and suffering can be caused by words/gestures/symbols/actions and ways in which conflicts can be avoided/lessened/resolved
Republic of Ireland	SPHE	• identify reasons for conflict in different situations • identify and discuss various responses to conflict situations and decide on and practise those that are the most appropriate or acceptable
Scotland	PSD	• discuss more than one strategy for coping with or tackling problems
Wales	PSE	• understand the situations which produce conflict • develop strategies to resolve conflict

Teacher information

The role-play cards on the following page should be cut out and given to pairs of students. The students must role-play the conflict they think will be caused by each situation. Teachers may like the students to choose a situation and perform it for the class, or may like the students to try out each role-play over several weeks, perhaps performing them for another pair.

Teachers should instruct the students to resolve the conflict they are role-playing. Students should also be encouraged not to make the role-plays screaming matches. The arguments used must be well-structured.

Discussion should follow the performances of the role-plays. This could include looking at reasons for the conflict starting, how each character dealt with it, what factors escalated it etc.

Encourage the students to use clear speech and gesture to show how the characters are feeling.

Discussion points

- Do you think the characters in this role-play found a fair solution to their problem?
- What were A's (or B's) reasons for beginning the conflict?
- How well did the characters in this role-play deal with the conflict?

Additional notes

Conflict role-plays

A and B are brothers/sisters.

A angrily accuses B of stepping on his/her favourite toy and breaking it. B refuses to apologise, saying that A shouldn't have left it lying around.

A and B are neighbours.

For the past three weeks, B has been playing the drums early on Sunday mornings when A likes to sleep in. A goes to talk to B about it.

A and B are shoppers.

A and B are in a busy bookshop, trying to buy a copy of a popular book. They pick up the last copy in the shop at the same time. They start to argue over who should get it.

A and B are brothers/sisters.

A and B both need to ring a friend in the next five minutes to say they are unable to meet them at the shops. A and B argue over who gets to use the phone to ring his/her friend first.

A and B are friends.

A and B are at a fair. A asks B to keep an eye on his/her bag while he/she goes to buy a drink. A starts to watch some fireworks and forgets. When B returns, the bag has disappeared.

A and B are friends.

A sees B cheating on a test, and tells their teacher. B gets into trouble. B has just found out who told the teacher. He/She angrily confronts A.

A and B are classmates.

A has been lying to B's friends, telling them that B has been saying horrible things about them. B has been wondering why his/her friends have been avoiding him/her. Then, one day, B overhears A lying.

A and B are strangers sitting next to each other at the cinema.

A and B have just finished watching a film. When the lights come up, B notices his/her wallet is missing. B accuses A of stealing it. A did not do it.

A and B are friends.

A gives B some money and asks him/her to buy a CD while B is at the shops. A accidentally buys the wrong CD. It cannot be returned.

A and B are friends.

A accidentally lets B's dog out into the street after being asked to shut the gate. The dog is almost hit by a car. B is very upset.

Conflict resolution skills – Conflict resolution evaluation

Activity objectives

- Describes and analyse a conflict situation.
- Identifies goals to resolve future conflicts more effectively.

Curriculum links

England	PSHE	• 2d know there are different kinds of responsibilities and rights at home/school/community, and that these can sometimes conflict with each other • 2f resolve differences by looking at alternatives, making decisions and explaining choices
Northern Ireland	PD	• know ways in which conflict and suffering can be caused by words/gestures/symbols/actions and ways in which conflicts can be avoided/lessened/resolved
Republic of Ireland	SPHE	• identify reasons for conflict in different situations • identify and discuss various responses to conflict situations and decide on and practise those that are the most appropriate or acceptable
Scotland	PSD	• discuss more than one strategy for coping with or tackling problems
Wales	PSE	• understand the situations which produce conflict • develop strategies to resolve conflict

Teacher information

As students begin to learn about conflict resolution, they will be attempting to break habits such as the two most common reactions to conflict—'flight' or 'fight'.

The conflict resolution steps can be reinforced by using the evaluation sheet on page 41. Initially, students may not complete any of the steps. As they become more familiar with the conflict resolution process, more of the evaluation sheet will be completed.

Ensure students complete Question 9. It is important that they consider what they could have done differently. File the sheets so that they can be brought out and discussed if a similar situation occurs.

Discussion points

- Why do you think an evaluation of a conflict situation is necessary? Isn't it better just to forget about it?
- Why might it be difficult to remember the conflict resolution steps when involved in a conflict?
- What happens to you physically when you are arguing with someone? (Temperature rises, flushed, clench fists, heart beats faster, sweat etc.)

Additional notes

Conflict resolution – evaluation

Name: _____ Class: _____ Date: _____

① Where were you when the conflict began?

② Who was involved in the conflict?

③ Who witnessed the conflict?

Steps Completed
1. Stop and cool off. ☐
2. Define the problem.
   • Use 'I' statements. ☐
   • Tell the other person what happened. ☐
   • Tell the other person how you feel. ☐
3. Brainstorm solutions. ☐
4. Choose a solution that is fair to both
   of you. (Compromise is the key!) ☐
5. Make a plan. Decide how you will
   put it into action. ☐
6. Agree to the plan. ☐

④ Describe what started the conflict.

_____

_____

⑤ Did you tell the other person what you think happened and how you were feeling?   ⊂ Yes ⊂ No ⊂

Explain. _____

_____

⑥ Did both parties brainstorm solutions to the problem?   ⊂ Yes ⊂ No ⊂

Explain. _____

_____

⑦ (a) Did you choose a solution that both parties thought was fair?   ⊂ Yes ⊂ No ⊂

(b) What was the chosen solution?

⑧ Did both parties agree to the solution?   ⊂ Yes ⊂ No ⊂

Did you make a plan?

⊂ Yes ⊂ No ⊂

Yes – Describe your plan.

No – What will you do next?

⑨ What will you do if faced with a similar situation in the future?

⑩ Signed

_____

Negotiation – What is negotiation?

Teacher information

Negotiation is a problem-solving process used to resolve conflict. The goal of negotiation is to create a solution that the conflicting parties agree to.

Before a negotiation meeting, the people involved should think carefully about what they will say. The parties then meet in a quiet, neutral place; e.g. a 'negotiating table' in a corner of the classroom. The conflict is identified and an agreement to resolve it is made.

Both parties then use 'I' statements to describe the problem from their point of view. After each person speaks, the other restates what he/she has heard to show he/she has understood. Solutions to the conflict are then brainstormed, and the best solution is agreed upon.

Effective negotiation relies on clear communication, problem-solving skills, showing respect and a focus on finding a 'win-win' solution.

Students should understand the concept of 'I' and 'You' statements before completing the activity on the following page.

After students have completed the questions, they could use their answers to role-play Jessie and Charlie's negotiation, using one of their brainstormed solutions. Either of the characters can be changed to girls if necessary. The role-plays should end with the characters agreeing to the chosen solution.

Discussion points

- Which features do you think an effective negotiator has? Could anyone learn to be an effective negotiator?
- What would hinder a successful negotiation?
- Why is it important to use 'I' statements?
- Why is it important to use 'You' statements?

Additional notes

What is negotiation?

Negotiation is a process whereby people in conflict meet to resolve their dispute.

- Before meeting, each person thinks about the conflict and what he/she wants.

- The two people meet. They state the problem and agree to try to solve it.

- Both people take turns to explain the problem, using 'I' statements. The listener uses 'You' statements to show he/she understands.

- Possible solutions are brainstormed.

- One solution is decided upon. Both agree to try it.

Working together to find a solution.

Be clear about what you need.

Remember your listening skills.

(1) Read this conflict scenario.

Jessie and Charlie are cousins who have decided to go on a holiday together. Unfortunately, they can't agree on where to go. Jessie would like to relax in a hotel at the beach but Charlie would like to go camping. Jessie doesn't want to camp because he did that last year. He also feels he needs a good break after working hard all year. Charlie thinks the hotel Jessie wants to stay at is too expensive and relaxing on the beach is boring.

(2) Answer the questions to show how Jessie and Charlie could use negotiation to solve their conflict.

(a) List Jessie's and Charlie's wants.

Jessie wants _____

Charlie wants _____

(b) Complete each sentence to make an 'I' statement Jessie or Charlie might use. After each, write a 'You' statement that the other person could respond with.

Jessie: I _____

Charlie: You _____

Jessie: I _____

Charlie: You _____

(3) Brainstorm two possible solutions to the conflict. Highlight the better one.

Negotiation – Discussing needs

Activity objectives

- Communicates wants and needs clearly.
- Listens carefully to others' wants and needs.
- Understands the importance of clear communication during negotiation.

Curriculum links

England	PSHE	• 2d know there are different kinds of responsibilities and rights at home/school/community, and that these can sometimes conflict with each other
		• 2f resolve differences by looking at alternatives, making decisions and explaining choices
Northern Ireland	PD	• know ways in which conflict and suffering can be caused by words/gestures/symbols/actions and ways in which conflicts can be avoided/lessened/resolved
Republic of Ireland	SPHE	• identify reasons for conflict in different situations
		• identify and discuss various responses to conflict situations and decide on and practise those that are the most appropriate or acceptable
Scotland	PSD	• discuss more than one strategy for coping with or tackling problems
Wales	PSE	• understand the situations which produce conflict
		• develop strategies to resolve conflict

Teacher information

Stating wants and needs is an important part of the negotiation process. Fair solutions to conflict can only be negotiated if both people understand what the other wants or needs.

When describing wants and needs, students should be encouraged to speak calmly and give reasons. When listening to someone else, they should demonstrate active listening through positive feedback and eye contact.

Students will need to work with a partner for the activity on the following page. Before the activity begins, each pair will need to decide who will play 'A' and who will play 'B'. The scenarios below can then be cut out and distributed. Instruct the students to look only at their own piece of paper.

Discussion points

- Why should you express your wants or needs calmly?
- Did you find it easy or difficult to listen to your partner's wants and needs? Explain.
- Why is it important to listen carefully to each other when you are negotiating?
- Why is it important to try to meet both sets of wants and needs when you are negotiating?

Additional notes

A *It is Sunday afternoon. You have just remembered that you haven't finished a school project that is due tomorrow. You race to the family computer, but your brother/sister is using it. He/She has been using it for two hours. You tell him/her to let you use the computer. He/She refuses.*

B *It is Sunday afternoon. You have been surfing the Internet on the family computer for two hours when your brother/sister interrupts you and tells you to let him/her use the computer. You are looking up information for a school project and you haven't finished yet. You refuse.*

Find a partner to work with. Read the scenario you are given. Don't look at your partner's!

Hear, don't just listen!

① List your wants and/or needs. Take turns to read aloud what you wrote.

② Write what you heard your partner say.

③ Did your partner listen to what you said? Colour the box that describes how well he/she understood.

ON FIRE	HOT	WARM	COLD	ICE-FORMING

If you chose 'Warm', 'Cold' or 'Ice-Forming', ask your partner to listen to you again. Make sure he/she clearly understands your wants or needs before you go any further!

④ Discuss with your partner how you think both sets of wants and needs could be met. Write the best solution you come up with.

_____

_____

_____

_____

⑤ Tick the box that best describes how you feel about this solution.

☐ overjoyed ☐ happy ☐ could be better ☐ unhappy ☐ miserable

Negotiation – Brainstorming solutions

Brainstorming solutions

1 Read the play script below.

Narrator: Anna and Jacob live next door to each other. Jacob has just bought a puppy called Casper. When Jacob is at work, Casper barks constantly. This disturbs Anna, who works from home. Casper also gets into Anna's backyard through a hole in the fence, where he chases her cat and digs up her garden. Anna has had enough. She meets with Jacob to negotiate some solutions to the problem. They discuss their feelings, then they begin to brainstorm some possible solutions ...

Anna: The first problem we need to talk about is the puppy barking all the time. It's difficult for me to concentrate when I'm trying to work.

Jacob: I was thinking about getting another dog to keep him company.

Anna looks horrified.

Jacob: But that could make the problem worse, I suppose.

Anna: What about taking Casper to obedience classes?

Jacob: I don't have time for that. I work long hours.

Anna: Well, what about leaving out some toys so he doesn't get bored when you are at work?

Jacob: That's a good idea, I'll try that.

Anna: If you like, I could also come over to play with the puppy for a few minutes each day.

Jacob: That sounds great! I'm sure Casper would love that! I will give you a key to the house.

Anna: Now, what about Casper getting into my backyard? He's scaring my cat and my garden is getting ruined.

Jacob: That's easy. All we need to do is fix the hole in the fence. I'm happy to pay for the materials, if you will help me fix it. How does tomorrow morning sound?

Anna: Yes, I'm happy to help. I'm glad we've sorted this out.

They shake hands.

2 Write your own negotiating play script on a separate sheet of paper. Some ideas are listed below.

> **Being able to solve problems is a very important skill.**

- *Two friends can't agree on what to buy another friend for his/her birthday.*

- *Two classmates have to work on a project together, but can't agree on how the work should be divided up.*

3 Perform your play script with a partner!

Negotiation – Problem-solving

Curriculum links

England	PSHE	• 2d know there are different kinds of responsibilities and rights at home/school/community, and that these can sometimes conflict with each other • 2f resolve differences by looking at alternatives, making decisions and explaining choices
Northern Ireland	PD	• know ways in which conflict and suffering can be caused by words/gestures/symbols/actions and ways in which conflicts can be avoided/lessened/resolved
Republic of Ireland	SPHE	• identify reasons for conflict in different situations • identify and discuss various responses to conflict situations and decide on and practise those that are the most appropriate or acceptable
Scotland	PSD	• discuss more than one strategy for coping with or tackling problems
Wales	PSE	• understand the situations which produce conflict • develop strategies to resolve conflict

Teacher information

Problem-solving is an important skill that can be used in a range of curriculum areas. The steps on the following page can be used to solve problems in various situations.

The solutions the students come up with could be discussed or role-played.

Discussion points

- Why is it important to come up with a 'win-win' solution to a conflict?
- Could you leave any of the problem-solving steps out? Why/Why not?
- When else could you use problem-solving steps?

Additional notes

Problem-solving

Most problems can be solved by following these simple steps.

To be a good negotiator you need to be a good problem solver.

- **Define the problem**

   Write a simple sentence which explains the conflict.

- **Brainstorm possible solutions**

   Use everyone's ideas, even if others don't agree with or like them. Keep going until you can't think of any more ideas.

- **Evaluate the ideas**

   Ask these questions about each idea: 'Is it unkind?', 'Is it unfair?', 'Is it dishonest?', 'What is likely to happen if we try that idea?'

- **Decide on a solution and carry it out**

   You should choose a 'win-win' solution.

(1) Find a partner. Use the problem-solving steps to find a fair solution to this conflict. Use the space underneath for your notes.

Grace and Sally are twins who are about to have a birthday. They have begged their parents to buy them a pet, which they have agreed to. Now the twins are arguing about what sort of pet they should get. Grace would like to get a dog so she can teach it tricks and take it for walks. She would prefer a big dog. Sally is frightened of big dogs. She would like a smaller, fluffy animal that she can cuddle, like a rabbit. Grace thinks that keeping animals in cages is cruel. Their parents will only buy one pet. What should they do?

Notes

Our chosen solution:

Negotiation – Problem-solving activities

Activity objective

- Solves problems using problem-solving steps.

Curriculum links

England	PSHE	• 2d know there are different kinds of responsibilities and rights at home/school/community, and that these can sometimes conflict with each other
		• 2f resolve differences by looking at alternatives, making decisions and explaining choices
Northern Ireland	PD	• know ways in which conflict and suffering can be caused by words/gestures/symbols/actions and ways in which conflicts can be avoided/lessened/resolved
Republic of Ireland	SPHE	• identify reasons for conflict in different situations
		• identify and discuss various responses to conflict situations and decide on and practise those that are the most appropriate or acceptable
Scotland	PSD	• discuss more than one strategy for coping with or tackling problems
Wales	PSE	• understand the situations which produce conflict
		• develop strategies to resolve conflict

Teacher information

Students will need to be familiar with the problem-solving steps described on page 49 before completing this activity. The page may be provided for students to refer to if teachers feel it is necessary.

For all the problems on the following page, students will need to write their solutions on a separate sheet of paper. The solutions and the process they used could then be discussed with the class.

The individual problems could be given to pairs of less able/confident students.

Discussion points

- What were some of the solutions you brainstormed but decided not to use? Why did you decide against them?
- Are you completely happy with your chosen solution? Why/Why not?
- Do you think there is a clear answer to the problem?

Additional notes

The coach (Pairs)

Use problem-solving steps to solve this problem.

You have both been doing gymnastics with the same coach for years. You have won many competitions and want to compete in the Olympics when you are older.

Then your coach leaves, and you get a new coach. Neither of you gets along with this new coach who is not encouraging, which, as a result, leads to you performing badly.

There is a competition coming up in a month, and you both want to do well. There are no other gymnastic schools near where you live and you cannot get your old coach back.

What do you do?

Second prize (Individual)

Use problem-solving steps to solve this problem.

Your class has entered a story-writing competition. Just before the results are announced, you overhear one of your classmates telling a friend that she copied her story from an old book.

Your classmate wins first prize. She wins some money and will meet your favourite author. You win second prize, for which you receive a certificate.

If you complain, you are afraid of looking like a sore loser. You think your classmate will lie anyway.

What do you do?

Injured bird (Pairs)

Use problem-solving steps to solve this problem.

You are friends out walking together when you see an injured bird.
You are near a phone booth, so you try to call the local wildlife carer, but there is no-one home. You have no more money for phone calls.

You are at least a 15-minute walk away from either of your houses. You know that none of your parents is at home. You are afraid to leave the bird in case a predator comes along.

What do you do?

Party time! (Individual)

Use problem-solving steps to solve this problem.

It is almost your birthday and you are planning a party. You want to invite 10 school friends, but there is a problem—two of your friends do not get along with each other. They had a huge argument a week ago and say they will never be friends again. They fight every time they see each other.

If you invite both of your friends, you know they will make your party unpleasant for everyone. You don't want to invite just one of them. You like them both equally and would love them to come to your party.

What do you do?

Negotiation – Evaluating negotiation

Activity objective

- Evaluates a negotiation in which he/she has taken part.

Curriculum links

England	PSHE	• 2d know there are different kinds of responsibilities and rights at home/school/community, and that these can sometimes conflict with each other
		• 2f resolve differences by looking at alternatives, making decisions and explaining choices
Northern Ireland	PD	• know ways in which conflict and suffering can be caused by words/gestures/symbols/actions and ways in which conflicts can be avoided/lessened/resolved
Republic of Ireland	SPHE	• identify reasons for conflict in different situations
		• identify and discuss various responses to conflict situations and decide on and practise those that are the most appropriate or acceptable
Scotland	PSD	• discuss more than one strategy for coping with or tackling problems
Wales	PSE	• understand the situations which produce conflict
		• develop strategies to resolve conflict

Teacher information

The following page can be given to students who have used negotiation to solve a conflict. Part 1 should be completed immediately after the negotiation. Part 2 should be completed after the students have had a chance to try out their chosen solution. This will vary according to the situation, but should be at least a few days afterwards.

Discussion point

- What did the evaluation sheet reveal about your negotiating skills?

Additional notes

Evaluating negotiation

Complete Part 1 immediately after your negotiation has taken place. Complete Part 2 after you have begun to try your chosen solution—perhaps a few days or a week later.

PART 1   Date _____

Name of children _____

Conflict _____

_____

Brainstormed ideas

Chosen solution _____

_____

I agree to this solution.   Signed _____   _____

During our negotiation ...

• we showed respect towards each other.   Yes ☐   No ☐

• we communicated well.   Yes ☐   No ☐

• the chosen solution was the best of our brainstormed ideas. Yes ☐   No ☐

PART 2   Date _____

Write how you both feel about the solution now. _____

_____

_____

If you feel the solution is not working, will you:

• *give it more time?* ☐   • *improve the solution?* ☐

• *go back to your list of brainstormed ideas?* ☐

Explain your decision. _____

_____

_____

Peer mediation – Peer mediation steps

- Reads and discusses peer mediation steps.

Curriculum links

England	PSHE	• 2d know there are different kinds of responsibilities and rights at home/school/community, and that these can sometimes conflict with each other • 2f resolve differences by looking at alternatives, making decisions and explaining choices
Northern Ireland	PD	• know ways in which conflict and suffering can be caused by words/gestures/symbols/actions and ways in which conflicts can be avoided/lessened/resolved
Republic of Ireland	SPHE	• identify reasons for conflict in different situations • identify and discuss various responses to conflict situations and decide on and practise those that are the most appropriate or acceptable
Scotland	PSD	• discuss more than one strategy for coping with or tackling problems
Wales	PSE	• understand the situations which produce conflict • develop strategies to resolve conflict

Teacher information:

Mediation is the process where a third, neutral party listens to both sides to resolve a conflict. It is based on the belief that resolutions are best reached with the help of a neutral third party and that children are more honest with and more likely to listen to peers than adults when discussing conflict. Common conflicts peer mediators face include name-calling, rumours, taking property without asking, teasing and invading personal space.

Peer mediation is usually most effective when the mediators are older primary students. However it is important that students should have observed the teacher mediate using similar steps and the students have had many opportunities to practise mediating before attempting to mediate themselves. Pre-mediation steps can be found in *Conflict Resolution Lower Primary*.

Peer mediators must be trained for a period of time before taking on the role. They are trained to attack the problem, rather than the people involved. They encourage the parties to treat each other with respect. During the discussion, each person is required to state the problem, describe his/her feelings and say how he/she is responsible for the problem. Possible solutions are then brainstormed, and a fair solution that suits both parties is reached. Solutions may require compromise from both parties.

A successful peer mediation programme can enhance communication and problem-solving skills, create a more comfortable school environment and encourage tolerance of others. It can also be empowering for students because they are assuming a greater responsibility for their own problems.

Peer mediation is in its infancy in terms of widespread practice in the UK and Ireland, but it is popular in the USA and Australia.

Peer mediation should only be attempted in a school where staff and students have attended a training course. Details of courses can be found on the Internet. Try typing 'school mediation courses' into a search engine.

The steps on page 55 are one format for aiding students in resolving conflicts. The students may feel more ownership if they make up a class set of steps in their own words. (See Appendix 1 on page 70 for a conflict resolution template.)

Discussion points

- When you have disagreements with your brother(s) or sister(s) at home, who helps to sort out the problems?
- Make a list and tally the students' responses. Are they surprised with the results?
- How do they do this? List any common steps on the board.
- When you have disagreements at school, who helps to sort out the problems?
- How do they do this? List any common steps on the board.
- Are there different ways to solve disputes?
- What common steps can you see?
- What are the advantages and disadvantages of mediators being peers and not teachers?
- What age do you think students should be to become a peer mediator?

Peer mediation steps

1 Ask the people involved in the conflict if they want to resolve the problem.

2 Find a private place to hold the mediation.

3 Explain the rules:
- Agree to listen to each other's opinions.
- No interrupting, yelling or put-downs.
- Always tell the truth.

4 Ask each person to explain the problem and describe how it makes him/her feel.

5 Rephrase what he/she said to you in your own words.

6 All people brainstorm as many solutions as possible.

7 Discuss each solution.

8 Choose a solution.
- This might involve each person compromising a little.

9 Both parties agree to the solution
- Show agreement, such as with a handshake or by signing an agreement form.

Peer mediation – Peer mediation – 1

Activity objectives

- Learns the peer mediation steps.
- Uses peer mediation steps to solve a problem.

Curriculum links

England	PSHE	• 2d know there are different kinds of responsibilities and rights at home/school/community, and that these can sometimes conflict with each other • 2f resolve differences by looking at alternatives, making decisions and explaining choices
Northern Ireland	PD	• know ways in which conflict and suffering can be caused by words/gestures/symbols/actions and ways in which conflicts can be avoided/lessened/resolved
Republic of Ireland	SPHE	• identify reasons for conflict in different situations • identify and discuss various responses to conflict situations and decide on and practise those that are the most appropriate or acceptable
Scotland	PSD	• discuss more than one strategy for coping with or tackling problems
Wales	PSE	• understand the situations which produce conflict • develop strategies to resolve conflict

Teacher information:

A good peer mediator:
- is thoroughly trained in the steps to help two people solve a problem,
- does not judge anyone's behaviour,
- listens to both sides of the story,
- uses a consistent approach to solving problems,
- is impartial (does not play favourites).

Pages 56 – 59 are to be used in conjunction with each other.

Students should read the scenario on page 57 and, using the peer mediation steps, attempt to solve the problem to the satisfaction of both parties. Students should evaluate the process.

Discussion points

- Discuss the mediation steps carefully with the students, making sure they understand each step.
- When you have disagreements at home and one of your parents has to mediate, who is the better 'mediator' – mum or dad ? Why?
- Have you encountered any situation such as that on page 57?
- How were the situations resolved to everyone's satisfaction?
- Were mediation steps used?
- Discuss other situations similar to that on page 57, repeating the steps until the students are very familiar with them.

Additional notes

> Read the scenario below, then use the peer mediation steps to resolve the conflict.

> Focus on the problem, not the people.

Shane, Brad and Sean were great mates. One Saturday when Sean had to go to visit his Nanna, Shane and Brad spent the day at Brad's house using the Playstation™, playing cricket and creating space monsters with his LEGO™.

The following Monday at school, Shane and Brad were very 'chummy', ignoring Sean and talking about the fun they had on Saturday. Sean was starting to feel left out.

① Ask ' _____?'

② Find a private place. Name a private place you could go. _____

③ What are the rules? List them. _____

_____

_____

④ List the problems and how each person feels.

Sean:	Shane and Brad:

⑤ Rewrite what each person said to you in your own words.

Sean: _____

_____

Shane and Brad: _____

_____

Teachers notes - Peer mediation -1 (continued)

Activity objectives

- Learns the peer mediation steps.
- Uses peer mediation steps to solve a problem.

Curriculum links

England	PSHE	• 2d know there are different kinds of responsibilities and rights at home/school/community, and that these can sometimes conflict with each other
		• 2f resolve differences by looking at alternatives, making decisions and explaining choices
Northern Ireland	PD	• know ways in which conflict and suffering can be caused by words/gestures/symbols/actions and ways in which conflicts can be avoided/lessened/resolved
Republic of Ireland	SPHE	• identify reasons for conflict in different situations
		• identify and discuss various responses to conflict situations and decide on and practise those that are the most appropriate or acceptable
Scotland	PSD	• discuss more than one strategy for coping with or tackling problems
Wales	PSE	• understand the situations which produce conflict
		• develop strategies to resolve conflict

Teacher information:

A good peer mediator:

- is thoroughly trained in the steps to help two people solve a problem,
- does not judge anyone's behaviour,
- listens to both sides of the story,
- uses a consistent approach to solving problems,
- is impartial (does not play favourites).

Pages 56 – 59 are to be used in conjunction with each other.

Students should read the scenario on page 57 and, using the peer mediation steps, attempt to solve the problem to the satisfaction of both parties. Students should evaluate the process.

Discussion points

- Discuss the mediation steps carefully with the students, making sure they understand each step.
- When you have disagreements at home and one of your parents has to mediate, who is the better 'mediator' – mum or dad ? Why?
- Have you encountered any situations such as that on page 57?
- How were the situations resolved to everyone's satisfaction?
- Were mediation steps used?
- Discuss other situations similar to that on page 57, repeating the steps until the students are very familiar with them.

Additional notes

6 What are some solutions you have discovered?

_____

_____

_____

_____

7 Which is the best solution you have discussed and chosen?

_____

8 Does anyone have to compromise? How? _____

_____

_____

9 Have both parties agreed to the solution? ⊂ Yes ⊂ No ⊂

10 How are you going to seal the agreement?

_____

_____

_____

Evaluate your use of the steps.

- _Were both parties happy with the solution?_ ⊂ Yes ⊂ No ⊂

- _Did anyone have to compromise? If so, who and how?_

_____

_____

- _Were any of the steps more difficult than the others? If so, which ones and how?_

_____

- _Do you think you are a good mediator or not?_

  ⊂ Yes ⊂ No ⊂

Peer mediation - Peer mediation - 2

Activity objective

- Demonstrates knowledge of peer mediation steps by writing a dialogue.

Curriculum links

England	PSHE	• 2d know there are different kinds of responsibilities and rights at home/school/community, and that these can sometimes conflict with each other • 2f resolve differences by looking at alternatives, making decisions and explaining choices
Northern Ireland	PD	• know ways in which conflict and suffering can be caused by words/gestures/symbols/actions and ways in which conflicts can be avoided/lessened/resolved
Republic of Ireland	SPHE	• identify reasons for conflict in different situations • identify and discuss various responses to conflict situations and decide on and practise those that are the most appropriate or acceptable
Scotland	PSD	• discuss more than one strategy for coping with or tackling problems
Wales	PSE	• understand the situations which produce conflict • develop strategies to resolve conflict

Teacher information

The students need to be familiar with the peer mediation steps before commencing this activity.

Students are to write the exact words said to complete the peer mediation process. Students may wish to complete this activity with a partner or in a small group. Students working with a partner or in small groups should take turns to enact the role of peer mediator. Students need to always keep in mind the qualities of a good peer mediator (see page 54). Students need to remember to label clearly who is speaking.

Students who feel confident enough may wish to perform their scenario as a play.

Discussion points

- Were there a number of different ways that the scenario could have been resolved to bring about the same result?
- Were there any particular words or phrases that you found helpful to use during the peer mediation process?
- Are there any advantages or disadvantages to resolving a conflict using peer mediation?
- Were both parties completely happy with the solution?
- Were both parties happy with your role as peer mediator? Did they have any suggestions as to how you could improve your role next time?

Additional activities

- Students may think of scenarios they have encountered and use the peer mediation process to show how the conflict was resolved.
- Students may illustrate how conflicts without peer mediation have escalated.
- Students may use the scenario given and show how it can escalate without peer mediation.
- After students have performed their scenarios, the audience may rate the role of the peer mediator. In this way the students may be able to improve their peer mediation skills.

Using the scenario below as a guide, write the exact dialogue to show the peer mediation process.

You will need to include the dialogue of both parties and the mediator.

Don't judge anyone's behaviour.

Charlotte and her best friend, Brittany, are the most popular girls in their class. They seem to always have the most fashionable hairstyles and clothes at the school discos and everyone seems to want to be in their 'group'.

One day when Carey is at the shopping centre with her mum, she sees Charlotte and Brittany take and hide some sweets in their school bags. They both glance up to see Carey watching them.

The next day at school, Carey notices Charlotte and Brittany whispering to another group of girls and looking at her. No-one comes to sit near her at break.

_____
_____
_____
_____
_____
_____
_____
_____
_____
_____
_____
_____
_____
_____
_____
_____
_____

Peer mediation - evaluation

Activity objective

- Identifies goals to improve peer mediation skills in the future.

Curriculum links

England	PSHE	• 2d know there are different kinds of responsibilities and rights at home/school/community, and that these can sometimes conflict with each other
		• 2f resolve differences by looking at alternatives, making decisions and explaining choices
Northern Ireland	PD	• know ways in which conflict and suffering can be caused by words/gestures/symbols/actions and ways in which conflicts can be avoided/lessened/resolved
Republic of Ireland	SPHE	• identify reasons for conflict in different situations
		• identify and discuss various responses to conflict situations and decide on and practise those that are the most appropriate or acceptable
Scotland	PSD	• discuss more than one strategy for coping with or tackling problems
Wales	PSE	• understand the situations which produce conflict
		• develop strategies to resolve conflict

Teacher information

A vital step in developing peer mediation skills is evaluation of the role after carrying out a conflict resolution process. This will allow students to see where they have made mistakes and improve their role as mediator. Not all students have the ability to be good peer mediators. Some students may find it difficult to be completely impartial in their role. Always select students to train as mediators based on the qualities below.

A good peer mediator:
- is thoroughly trained in the steps to help two people solve a problem,
- does not judge anyone's behaviour,
- listens to both sides of the story,
- uses a consistent approach to solving problems,
- is impartial (does not play favourites).

After a student has completed a mediation process, evaluate his/her performance.

Discussion points

- Do you think that you have the qualities to be a good peer mediator? Yes/No? Why/Why not?
- Did you notice any steps that you found difficult? What were they? Why did you find them difficult?
- Can you name anyone in the class whom you think deserves to be a peer mediator? Why did you select him/her?
- What are some areas where you can improve your skills? How can you do this?
- What factors may contribute to making a peer mediation unsuccessful?
- Are there any helpful hints that you could give to others who are to take on the role of peer mediator?

Additional notes

① How did you hear about the conflict?

② How did you get involved?

③ Where did you go to hold the mediation?

④ Did you explain the rules clearly ? **Yes No** Do you think that both parties understood the rules correctly? **Yes No**

⑤ Do you think that both parties were able to explain their problems clearly enough? **Yes No**

⑥ Were there any difficulties? If so, where and why?

⑦ Did everyone suggest ideas for the solutions? **Yes No** Were there lots of ideas or only a few? Explain.

⑧ Did you discuss each solution fully? **Yes No** Were both parties listening with an open mind? **Yes No**

⑨ Did the chosen solution suit both parties? **Yes No** Did anyone have to compromise? Give details.

⑩ How did both parties show their agreement to the solution?

• *List some ways that you could improve your mediation skills.*

_____

_____

_____

Peace – Peaceful lake?

- Gains an understanding that peace depends on action and communication.
- Suggests some ways peace can be created.

Curriculum links

England	PSHE	• 4c develop skills to be effective in relationships
Northern Ireland	PD	• know ways in which conflict and suffering can be caused by words/gestures/symbols/actions and ways in which conflicts can be avoided/lessened/resolved
Republic of Ireland	SPHE	• identify reasons for conflict in different situations • discuss/explore concept of co-operating and ways this can be put into practice in an effective manner
Scotland	PSD	• discuss more than one strategy for coping with or tackling problems
Wales	PSE	• develop strategies to resolve conflict • work cooperatively to tackle problems

Teacher information

Peace is often thought of as a passive state—a lack of war. But peace is a process which requires action to be started and sustained. Obstacles to peace include fear of the unknown or the unfamiliar.

Each student will need to choose a partner for this activity. Before the pairs begin the activity, they must decide who will be chief of the Akari clan and who will be chief of the Mitta clan. As well as the activity sheet on the following page, each student will need a copy of the description of his/her clan below. It is important that each student does not read his/her partner's description at any time. The success of the activity relies on the students communicating with each other to achieve peace.

Discussion points

- What are some ways you could promote peace in your school or community?
- Discuss obstacles to peace and how they could be overcome; e.g. different values or beliefs.

Akari clan

Food – your clan eats mainly fish from the lake. You are so successful at catching fish that you often have too much for your tribe to eat. You also eat the only plant that grows on your side of the lake but it does not have a pleasant taste. There are many different plants growing on the Mitta's side of the lake that they eat. You have tried to sneak across the lake to steal some but they always catch you out.

Boating – canoeing is an important part of your culture and you need to teach the clan's children the skills needed. However, every morning you try, the Mittas are on the lake making lots of noise. This distracts the children.

Bathing – your clan bathes in the lake every day at different times. The Mittas are sometimes there when you are. They seem angry about this, although you don't know why.

- *You want the lake to yourself in the morning and at sunset every day. You are happy to share the lake with the Mittas at any other time.*

Mitta clan

Food – your clan eats mostly plants. This is because you are terrible at fishing. You notice that the Akaris catch a lot of fish they don't always eat. You have tried to sneak across the lake to steal some but they always catch you out.

Boating – you hold noisy races every morning just for fun.

Bathing – Your clan bathes in the lake every afternoon. This is a problem because sometimes the Akaris are also there. You don't like this because your clan believes that strangers should not watch you bathe.

- *You want the lake to yourself only when you bathe in the afternoons. You are happy to share the lake with the Akaris at any other time.*

Peaceful lake?

Quirri Lake is a large lake. Two clans live on opposite sides of it. Unfortunately, they are often in conflict because of their differences.

Imagine you and your partner have become the new chiefs of the two clans. You would like to live in peace with one another. You both know this will not just happen—it will take some action.

(1) **Read the description of your clan.**

NB – Do not read the description of your partner's clan.

(2) You and the other chief agree to meet to discuss how you can live in peace. Before you meet, answer these questions.

(a) Why is peace important to you? _____

_____

(b) Write your clan's needs and wants and any questions you would like to ask the other chief.

Needs and Wants	Questions

(3) Use your answers to help you discuss with the other chief how to create peace. You may need to look at your clan description again to help you answer questions the other chief asks you.

(4) Write how you would create peace between your clans. Report to the class.

Peace – What does peace mean to you?

Activity objective

- Defines the concept of peace.

Curriculum links

England	PSHE	• 2e reflect on moral and social issues
Northern Ireland	PD	• express their views
Republic of Ireland	SPHE	• identify the behaviour that is important for harmony
Scotland	PSD	• communicate with others through a developing vocabulary relating to emotions and feelings
Wales	PSE	• know and understand the range of their own feelings and emotions

Teacher information

When conflict is resolved, peaceful classrooms, schools, communities and countries can be the ultimate result. Individuals define the concept of peace in their own way. To some students this may be defined by being in a specific place, participating in a particular activity that makes them feel peaceful, or the feelings they have when listening to a piece to music or viewing a peaceful scene, painting or colour. To many, the feeling of peace may be defined as an absence of conflict—no worries, everything being calm.

In the present world climate, teachers should not distress students by dwelling on the wars within and between countries. Rather, they should emphasise resolving conflicts at all levels to reach a peaceful solution where everyone wins. Emphasise communication and its importance to peace.

Discussion points

- What does peace mean to you?
- When do you feel peaceful?
- Is there a special place that makes you feel peaceful?
- Can other people make you feel peaceful? If so, what kind of people are they?
- Why is peace important?
- What colours make you feel peaceful? Why do you think these colours make you feel peaceful?
- Do you listen to any music/sounds that make you feel peaceful?
- What is the opposite of peace?

Additional activities

- Find some symbols of peace.
- Design a poster promoting peace in the school or classroom.
- Research some famous people who tried to bring peace to their country or to the world.
- Create a dance using soft, gentle movements to accompany a peaceful piece of music.
- Write peace messages to send to a friend/'buddy'.

Additional notes

What does peace mean to you?

① Complete the sentences below.

(a) *'I feel peaceful when* _____

_____

_____

_____

(b) *'The most peaceful place I know is* _____

because _____

_____

② A dictionary meaning of 'peace' is _____

_____

③ Write some other words that mean peace.

④ Use the space below to design a poster to promote peace in your classroom or school.

We can all try to live peacefully in our little part of the world.

Tolerance – What is tolerance?

Activity objectives

- Recognises and values differences in individuals.
- Recognises and understands the need for tolerance.

Curriculum links

England	PSHE	• 4c develop skills to be effective in relationships
Northern Ireland	PD	• recognise real friendship and how to support peers in a positive way
Republic of Ireland	SPHE	• respect and show consideration for others
		• be aware of the importance of mutual respect and sensitivity of others
Scotland	PSD	• demonstrate respect and tolerance towards others
Wales	PSE	• respect others and value uniqueness
		• value and celebrate cultural difference and diversity
		• recognise uniqueness of individuals

Teacher information

We live in a multicultural society. We look different. We live differently. We have different types of families. Differences can enhance our relationships and enrich our society. Students need to be taught to recognise, appreciate and tolerate differences.

Tolerance is a skill which can reduce conflict and the need for conflict resolution. It is an on-going process.

Teaching tolerance is also teaching students not to hate. Teachers can teach tolerance most effectively by modelling tolerant behaviour in the classroom and playground. Students should be exposed to people, literature and images that are multicultural and which teach them about other faiths, ethnicities and lifestyles.

Educating students to be tolerant will:
- promote the understanding and acceptance of individual differences,
- minimise generalisations and stereotyping,
- help students to understand and appreciate the differences between people,
- highlight the need to combat prejudice and discrimination.

The student activity is intended to help students realise that we can appreciate each other's differences and that these differences can enrich our lives. Students may wish to illustrate their answers as well as write their answers.

Discussion points

- Why do people look different/the same?
- What foods do you like to eat that originated in another country?
- Were you born here? Were your parents? If not, where were they born?
- Do you follow any traditions/customs at your house which may be different from those of other people?
- Why is tolerance important? Does it mean that you have to agree with other people's beliefs?
- Would more tolerance make a difference to conflict in the classroom, school or world?

Additional activities

- Survey the students in your class. Note the same hair colour, eye colour, country of birth, faiths, favourite foods, favourite music etc.
- List ways of showing tolerance for other people.
- Write a poem/story about tolerance for/about someone who has no tolerance.
- Write a short play/skit about being tolerant of a new class member.

What is tolerance?

1. Using the members of your class, find a person who fits each category below:

a person who is taller than you	a person who has the same hair colour as you	a person who has the same number of children in the family as you	a person who was born in another country
a person whose favourite band is the same as yours	a person whose favourite food is the same as yours	a person who wears his/her hair the same as yours	a person who has a brother/sister with the same name as yours
a person who is exactly the same size as you	a person whose mother's name is the same as your mother's name	a person who wants to have the same job as you when he/she grows up	a person whose dad does the same job as yours

2. Why is it important to be tolerant of other people? _____

_____

_____

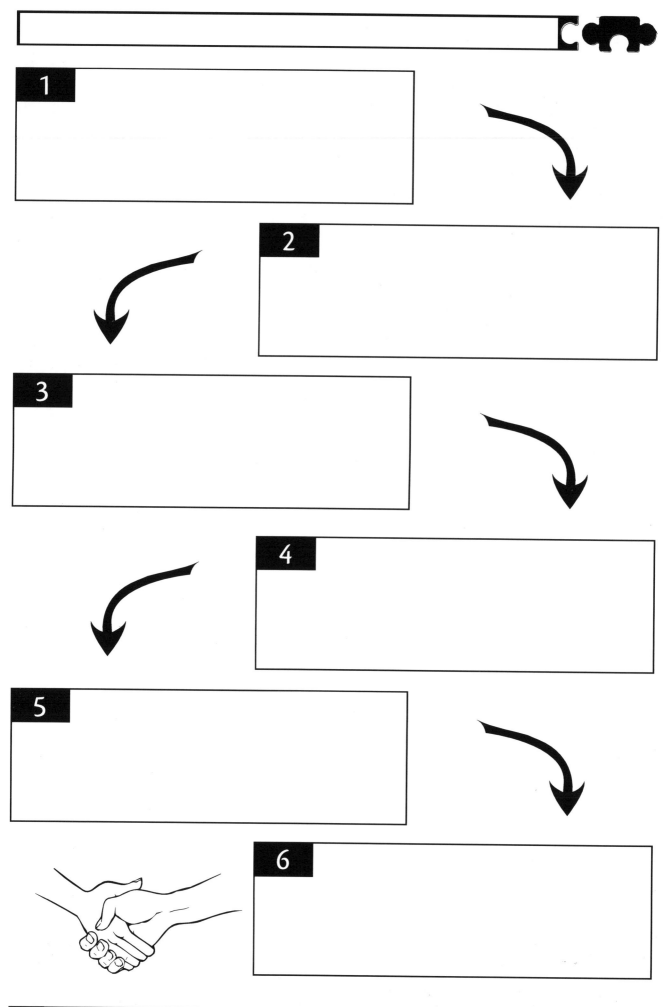